PURE RALLY

IT'S NOT ABOUT THE SETBACK,
IT'S ABOUT THE COMEBACK.

DR. ROB BELL

Cover Design: Fuel VM fuelvm.com
Interior Design: FormattedBooks.com

ISBN: 978-1-7343588-0-3 (Hardback)
ISBN: 978-1-7343588-1-0 (Paperback)
ISBN: 978-1-7343588-2-7 (E-book)

Published by: DRB Press

PUKE & RALLY

It's not about the SETBACK,
it's about the COMEBACK.

Dr. Rob Bell

ALSO BY DR. ROB BELL

Mental Toughness Training for Golf

The Hinge: The Importance of Mental Toughness

NO FEAR: A Simple Guide to Mental Toughness

Don't "Should" on Your Kids: Build Their Mental Toughness

50 Ways to Win: Pro Football's Hinge Moments

NO ONE Gets There ALONE

Follow PUKE & RALLY

Pukeandrallybook.com

www.facebook.com/TheImportanceofmentaltoughness/

#PUKEANDRALLY
@drrobbell drrobbell.com

#PUKEANDRALLY
@drrobbell

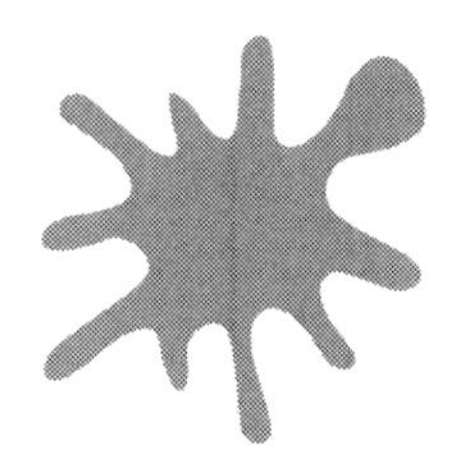

ADVANCED PRAISE

"We all experience failure and setbacks in our lives. But the truly successful people are those who take these negative experiences and turn them into a positive learning opportunity. In Puke & Rally, Dr. Rob Bell provides a mental framework you can use to overcome any challenge that life throws your way. Whether you're facing a personal or professional obstacle, this book will help you meet this challenge head on, learn from this experience, and then emerge as a stronger, tougher person."

—Steve Scott, author of Habit Stacking

"In this smart, fast-moving book, Dr. Rob Bell lays the foundation to help you get up, get going, and get ahead no matter what life or business throws your way. If you're looking to upgrade your career, your business, and your results–look no further. The resilience and mental toughness handbook for the rest of us is here. Buy a copy for everyone on your team. Yes, it's that good."

—David Newman, CSP,
author of "Do It! Marketing" and "Do It! Speaking

"I feel so sharp and ready to compete after reading PUKE & RALLY. I feel this way about Dr. Rob because the way he constantly walks the walk is inspiring."

—Adam Schenk, PGA Tour

"I became the Last Human Standing at the notorious, Big's Backyard Ultra, through a lot of epic failures. Behind every success is a whole lot of 'puking.' What makes all the difference is the 'rally.' Dr. Rob dissects the PUKE & RALLY phenomenon and lights a fire at the same time. You can't walk away from this read and not be inspired."

—Maggie Guterl, Winner 2019 Big's Backyard Ultra

"When I won my first PGA Tour event, Dr. Rob also completed a 50-mile ultra that same weekend. So, I wasn't going to let him get all the glory. Puke & Rally is the calling card to success because if you want something bad enough, you'll encounter setbacks. The key is 'will you comeback?'"

—Tyler Duncan, PGA Tour

"There will be major setbacks on our journey. But as Dr. Rob writes in PUKE & Rally, the process is more important than the product! It's about who we transform into because of the trials that we'll encounter and overcome."

—Martin Rooney, Coach, and
Best Selling Author of *Coach To Coach*

"I've interviewed hundreds of millionaires on my podcast and setbacks are common amongst them all. Failure is an asset. It is a gift that will direct us toward the correct path in our life. As Dr. Rob writes in PUKE & RALLY, failure is painful, but the required ingredient is how we respond to the adversity. It's all about the comeback!"

—Jaime Masters, *Eventual Millionaire*

"Dr Rob's new book Puke & Rally needs to be on all bookshelves. It gives you tactical ways to look at the problem and rise up against all odds. If you are searching for a book that will lift you up, help you find the inner strength you need to make a comeback, this is for you!"

—Devan Kline, CEO, Burn Boot Camp

"This is THE book about mental toughness I have always wanted to read. Dr. Bell's book is sharp, articulate and full of heart."

—John Brubaker,
Leadership Performance Expert, CoachBru.com

"I've been able to use my platform to inspire and touch lives. Thank you Dr. Rob Bell, may 'Puke & Rally' always be my battle cry!"

—Sandy Zimmerman, Inaugural mother to
hit the Buzzer on American Ninja Warrior

"Puke and Rally is another stellar example of Rob Bell's ability to creatively describe life's obstacles and provide ideas that will help us respond to adversity."

—Joe Skovron, PGA Tour caddy

"Life is not a marathon as Dr. Rob writes in PUKE & Rally. It's more like a 100-mile trail race, I know, I've done them! Life is hard and unless we make up our mind to never give up, then eventually we will quit. However, if we can focus correctly and have confidence and courage, then we can create our comeback!"

—Lisa Tamati, Coach, and author of *Relentless*

"Being successful in life isn't about what you achieve, but your ability to look adversity in its dark eyes and move past it. Puke & Rally shows us that everyone "pukes" at some stage of their life, but it's about those who are able to comeback from the painful setbacks! Dr. Rob Bell once again has written an insightful, educating, and relatable book that we all can learn from!"

—Luke Tyburski, *The Ultimate Triathlon*,
Author of *Chasing Extreme*

"The title of Dr. Rob Bell's latest book sums up the secret to success in life. Learn how to "PUKE" your setbacks and use life's trials as a force multiplier to "RALLY" back and propel your life positively forward. Puke & Rally will confidently guide you through parable after the parable of historical examples to PROVE to you that you too can "PUKE AND RALLY". Embrace the journey!"

—Dan Hawkins, Head Football Coach,
University of California, Davis

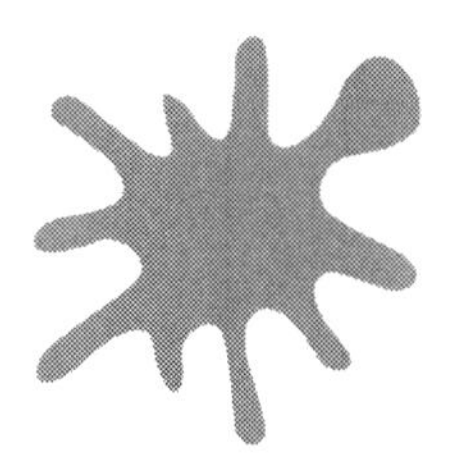

ACKNOWLEDGEMENTS

To my family, Nicole, Ryan, and Porter, who live through it all. I simply could not have done it without you.

Mike Madrid and Highway Safety Services for their support and sponsorship of the book.

Andrew Curtis and FuelVM for their book design and tireless contributions.

Aly Fuller, Will Drumright, Sam Engel, Brandon Danker, and Mary and Mitch Towe, for their support and help along the arduous journey. To Joe Merz, Michael Sachs, Leslee Fisher, and Craig Wrisberg.

To my entire professional, corporate, collegiate, and high school athletes. You provide purpose and meaning in being able to coach and guide you to success and significance. Your willingness to constantly improve motivates me everyday. I am blessed to be around and interact with so many great people.

Thank you to all of the great coaches that I have learned from and worked along side. You make such a difference in people's lives.

To those who help contribute their stories by sharing and living life to the fullest: Larry Jackson, Derick Grant, Brooks Williams, Devan and Morgan Kline, Lindsey Stirling, Diana Nyad, Sonja Bennett, Brett Favre, and Bronnie Ware.

Your Free Gift(s)

As a way of saying "thank-you" for purchasing this book, PUKE & RALLY, I wanted to offer my readers a free download.

8 Ways to Puke & Rally Infographic
pukeandrallybook.com/infographic

Want to see what type of personality it takes
to PUKE & RALLY? Take the Quiz.

PUKE & RALLY QUIZ
Pukeandrallybook.com/quiz

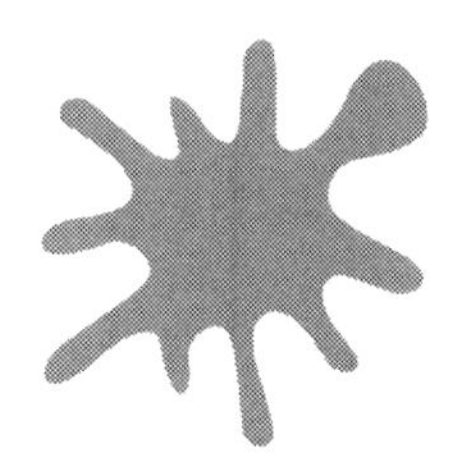

FOREWORD

I WAS ONE of the 72 million people in North America who saw The Beatles perform on the Ed Sullivan TV show in 1964. I was only 10 years old and that experience blew me away.

It was at that Hinge moment that I realized my purpose in life was to play the drums in a Rock 'n' Roll band, make records and tour the world.

Seventeen years later at age 27 I finally got my big break when I won an audition to play drums for a new young artist, Johnny Cougar (John Cougar Mellencamp). Five weeks later we flew to Los Angeles to make a record. I told everyone that I finally made it. My dream had become my reality. I was ecstatic, elated and excited.

But after two days of recording we had a band meeting, and in that meeting John told me *"You're not playing on the record and you should fly home to Bloomington, IN."* I was devastated, crushed, ashamed, fearful and overwhelmed. The truth was, I had no experience making hit records and the producer wanted a session drummer who had experience making hit records.

Without thinking, and from a place of *fight or fight,* not fight or flight, I said *"NO!! I'm not going home."* I told John I wanted to stay in Los Angeles and go to the studio and watch the other drummers record my drum parts. Finally, I said, *"and you don't have to pay me."* That sealed the deal.

I had to fight for my purpose and dream and for four weeks, I watched, and asked questions of the two other drummers. I learned a lot in those four weeks and put together a new plan and new approach to serving Johnny Cougar and his music. I made a vow to myself that I would be the drummer on his next record.

Two years later I was in Criteria Recording Studios in Miami making John's next record. It was one of the most difficult records I have ever made, but one year later that record *American Fool* won two Grammies and John had his most successful #1 hit single in his career *Jack and Diane*, which featured me on drums.

His career blew up and my career took off. I spent 17 years recording and touring with John Mellencamp and since *American Fool,* I have recorded over 60 Grammy-nominated or awarded records representing over 300 million in sales, with more than 1,300 that were RIAA certified Gold, Platinum or Diamond.

I had to Puke and Rally my entire life.

I don't believe in failing or making mistakes. Dr. Bell is correct, "It's not about the setback." Those experiences are in fact "gifts" to becoming the best version of yourself. "It's about the comeback!" However, if you do nothing, you get nothing. Take Action!! Puke & Rally!

—Kenny Aronoff, Drummer Hall of Fame

Puke (verb)

Vomit

Rally (verb)

A mustering of scattered forces to renew an effort. A summoning up of strength or courage after weakness or dejection. A renewed offensive.

Setback (Noun)

To slow the progress of.

Comeback (Noun)

To recover from a deficit in a contest or competition.

HOW WE PUKE

"Champions before championships."—Anonymous

I WAS GOING to attempt a 50-kilometer trail run.

This trail run took place in the mountains and was known for its difficulty in elevation change and also because of the muddy and off-balance terrain throughout.

The race itself offered a few options for distances. Most people sign up for the "toughest 10k in the nation", a well-deserved nickname. And in addition to the 50k race, there was also a 50-mile race.

A bit of perspective about the difficulty of the hilly race terrain was that one finisher described the 50-miler as being more difficult than a 100-miler that he had previously completed.

There were a few negative marks against me heading into the race.

Living in the awesome city of Indianapolis unfortunately provides a dearth of any type of hills to train on. We perform like we train, and running on flat surfaces does not prepare one for a hilly off-road race. The second stain against me was my actual preparation for this ultra-marathon. I hurt my Achilles tendon training so I was as ready as someone who crams the night before for a final exam.

The third mark against me was the time of year. It was held in May, which is a beautiful time of year, but spring missed us completely. The week before the race, the *high* temperature was still in the 40s. It went straight to summer the exact day of the race and the temperature reached the 80s.

The first 15 miles of the race went well. The hills were tough but manageable and the cloud cover made it cool. I enjoyed the scenery and conversing with a group of fellow runners. However, after the half-marathon distance, warning lights started to go off.

The clouds burned off and it was direct sun, which caused it to warm up quickly. My legs started to tire enough that I was now walking the steep hills that I had not properly prepared for.

I hit a much-needed rest stop at mile twenty and knew I needed to reset. The rest stops at ultra-races are sometimes stocked to the gills with anything you could possibly want. It's sort of like a tailgate for a football game, except for the beer of course.

The rest stop had water, coke, mountain dew, watermelon, cookies, cakes, candy, nuts, pretzels, potato chips—everything.

I didn't know it at that exact moment, but my body was in severe dehydration mode. When this happens, the blood sugar in your body goes a bit haywire, causing some major issues. Blood sugar fuels the muscles, so the body pulls it away from the stomach, leaving nothing behind to digest food. My body could no longer break down any solid food entering the body.

This is why it's so important to prevent dehydration, because once you're in that physiological state, it's often too late to recover well.

Well, I was not thinking about my precise dehydration as I sat in the chair at the rest stop.

I needed to recharge and reset. At the same time, everything on the table looked so good, I was like a junkie running dry and looking for a fix.

So I decided to try it all. Just searching for anything to help me refuel and recharge and feel better.

First, the Mountain Dew® and Gatorade®, followed by some Fig Newtons®. The pretzels looked appealing because of the salt, and I also thought the Peanut M&M's would be tasty along with Trail Mix. While I was at it, I always liked Twizzlers® too.

By this point, it was midday so the sun was at its highest and we all could seriously feel the heat and humidity. I knew my family would be waiting for me at mile 24, just four hilly miles away. My thought process was, *"just make it there."*

Then, from there, I knew it was eight hilly miles to the finish line, twelve miles in total.

After my free buffet at mile 20, I took off down the single-track trail, determined to make it.

However, I had barely made it a mile straight down into the deep woods when I experienced plain shutdown mode. In trail races, when you make it to the forest floor, you know there is always an uphill to follow. There is something about physics that supports that claim.

Severe shutdown mode began with me sitting on the side of a steep uphill. Every 30 seconds or so, I'd get up, stagger forward a few hundred yards and sit down again. Fellow racers were passing me with everyone saying the same thing, *"Are you okay, do you need anything?"* It was not good.

I needed to vomit and I did. Bam, it provided immediate relief!

I was now back up on my feet and moving forward. However, this feel-good vacation from having puked lasted about ten minutes. I was at the bottom of a final climb, a mere ¼ mile from the next rest stop and where my family would be, when disaster struck.

I puked again.

But this time, it all came up. It was projectile. The session lasted a few minutes. The red Twizzlers® also seemed to don everything colorfully. But, I finally made it to the top of the hill at mile 24, feeling okay once again.

This "okay" feeling wouldn't last either.

I needed to rehydrate. Except that I had passed the point of no return and when I drank any fluids, it almost immediately came back up.

My kids, nine and seven years old at the time, were with their mother, my wife, and they all witnessed this happening. As you can imagine, they were in tears because they had never seen their dad in a state of complete collapse before.

The volunteers at the rest stop and my wife were pointing out my sunken eyes and skin discoloration. She was adamant about pulling me from the race, but I was determined to keep going. I suggested a compromise, like an extended break.

I was not going to quit.

Even though it was 80+ degrees, I was experiencing heat exhaustion, dehydration, and I got the chills. Not a good sign.

Just as all of this hectic mess was occurring, the skies opened up. It was not a summer drizzle either, it was a downpour, and the kind where you are soaked in a manner of seconds.

It was tough for me to even think clearly. I retreated along with my family to our truck.

My vomiting persisted and I would open the door in the backseat to the downpour going on, projectile vomit outside, and close the door again. I have no idea how more can come back up than I ever put down! My kids were still sobbing at this point unable to process what was occurring.

Vomiting, having the chills, and an epic downpour is a cocktail for dropping out.

My wife informed the race officials at the aid station, *"He's stopping."* Funny, but later my wife mentioned how the officials commented that a lot of runners had done the same thing.

My race was done.

My wife drove us back to the cabin that we were renting. It was like I was ill, I had major chills and dry heaves, so I sat in the shower and tried to warm up.

I made it to the bed shivering, and passed out. I slept for probably 30 minutes or so, and as I woke and lay in bed my head was filled with thoughts of failure. I heard my son innocently ask on the ride back to the cabin, *"You mean daddy HAD to quit?"*

The negative voice inside of me was yelling at me, "*So what, you were throwing up?*" "*You keep moving and don't give up, but you went and gave up!*" The negativity that I felt from messing up was awful. It's at times like these that we seem to conjure up all of our past failures from our entire lives.

Another 30 minutes or so passed and I managed to get myself outside to the porch. I took my time, but carefully ate some food and sipped on some water.

It became a *"Who are you?"* moment.

Sure, other people would understand why I dropped out, but that didn't matter. Could I look myself in the eye and tell other people, my clients, my athletes, and my kids to never give up, when I had, in fact, done just that?

The food stayed down so I had some more water. I started to get my second wind and my thoughts shifted from *"Why didn't you finish" to "I need to finish."*

One of my PGA Tour winners always had an epic saying. When faced with a difficult decision, his default mode was to be aggressive. He would say, *"We didn't come here to paint."* It meant that he came to do a job and finish it.

My family had all fallen asleep, but I woke them up from their slumber and told them, *"We are going back."* My wife, God bless her, knew I was serious, so we hustled back to the rest stop where I had stopped and informed the officials that I was returning. I had just made the last cut-off time before they pull runners from the course.

Two and half-hours after I initially dropped out, I checked back in with the race officials exactly where I had stopped and went to finish my race.

It had stopped raining an hour before, so now it was hot, muddy, and the forest flies were massive. But I joined up with another 50-mile racer about a mile into the deep forest and we helped each other finish the final eight miles of the race.

I finished last.

It was fitting, but it so happens that I was the only name on the last results page. No one has broken that slow record time yet, but I finished. It was still faster than the people who dropped out of the race and never returned.

Puke
&
Rally.

The appropriate thing about sporting contests is that it gives us the test first and we get the lesson afterwards. Life and school are not like that; we do not show up to class the very first day and take the final exam.

For some, entering such an endurance race is unthinkable. For others, finishing would have been an afterthought after suffering with those intestinal issues.

However, commitment is the same concept regardless of our chosen endeavor. It means finishing what we started, no matter how bad the situation or the circumstances. Commitment means continuing to press on, long after the mood in which we made the commitment has worn off.

My belief is that you do not give up, no matter what!

Of course, a major injury or life-threatening situation would have been different. But this was a temporary setback. It may sound selfish, but I was actually thinking of my family when I answered that question of *"Who are you?"* I want them to be as passionate about their own journey and be willing to push themselves past their own barriers and limitations.

If you've seen the video of Will Smith discussing his level of commitment and running on a treadmill, he echoes this same point. *"You might have more talent than me, you may be smarter than me, but if we get on a treadmill together, one of two things are going to happen: either you're getting off first, or I'm gonna die on that treadmill."*

It sounds tough, and with Will Smith, it is a truism. That is why he is one of the best actors ever.

There are people who overcome some insane challenges and obstacles in life. They live on the edge of life and Puke & Rally is their cry. They possess an unwillingness to give up.

Many call it crazy, but crazy is what creates the coolest stuff.

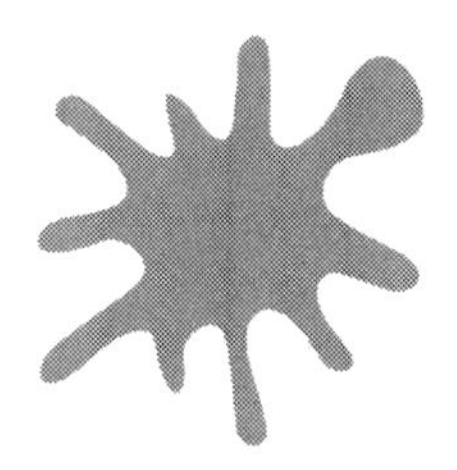

WE'VE ALL THROWN UP

VOMITING IS NOT fun, but it's necessary.

It's our body's natural response to get rid of nasty toxins, whether it's alcohol, food poisoning, endurance races, or extreme exercise. Some medications or health conditions can cause vomiting. Travel such as motion sickness can cause us to retch. A woman's morning sickness from pregnancy can cause extreme nausea.

We could even have gratitude for it. We sometimes feel better having gone through it. But throwing up is a special ability that not all animals possess. For instance, mice simply lack the ability to throw up, which is why rat poison is so effective.

Vomiting is also sometimes a sign that *"You're ready."*

I've known several professional and collegiate athletes who would heave before playing, and it was actually a good thing for them.

During the first inning versus the Texas Rangers, Adrian Houser was pitching for the Milwaukee Brewers. He unfortunately booted a ball hit directly back to him. Shortly after the error, he doubled over and hurled directly onto the infield. His violent puke caused the athletic trainers to come running and the infielders to surround him. But, once that affair was finished, he rallied!

He pitched six innings, allowed only one run, and struck out 10 batters en route to the win.

Puke
&
Rally.

Sometimes "tossing your cookies" is voluntary because it's the only option.

My wife would experience migraines so severe that she needed to relieve the vice-grip pressure in her head. She would engage her gag reflex and voluntarily heave. It was impressive to do so on command, but it would be the only relief to her severe pain.

Vomiting is also a rite of passage.

Many have ridden an amusement park ride so many times in a row that they've hurled, or got close. As kids growing up, we held just enough responsibility to make poor choices at the fair or carnival. Not knowing the limit of how many times one can ride the tilt-a-whirl is the confidence of youth. Once we did retch though, we never looked at the ride in quite the same way, but we learned.

Other times, we'll do anything to avoid puking. It is no fun, so we take something to relieve the nausea.

I'm sure few actually enjoy puking, but I hated it. As a kid, I'd start to pray immediately to not throw-up and even asked why God allowed us to throw-up. Thinking it was the end of the civilization as we know it, and to a kid feeling ill it was.

Little did I know that this theme of puking would present itself in my professional career as well.

My first full 140.6 Ironman (2.4 mile swim, 112 mile bike, and 26.2 mile run) was on the eastern shore in Maryland. It was beautiful but very warm that day, and yes, I puked at mile 16 of the marathon. But, I still finished.

At the same 50k race a year later, I again had to puke and rally as I became ill just three miles from the end. But, I still finished.

I hope I'm not crushing anyone's epic hopes here, but this is not a book about being a fifth-year undergrad student and extending your weekend celebrations. This is also not a "how-to" guide for sport coaches about getting your athletes *tougher* by having them throw up at practices.

This is a book that identifies with what we have all been through at some point. We will all puke in life, and it's not about the setbacks in our life, but about the comebacks! Being a champion in any area of your life will require you to Puke & Rally.

SPOILER ALERT: LIFE HAS SETBACKS

> *"Life is not always about what you have, it's about what you have left."*—Robert Schuller

Setback (Noun)
To slow the progress of.

MOST SELF-HELP BOOKS tout five ways to success or three simple steps to fulfillment. It's frankly all crap.

Life is hard!

Success is not guaranteed.

Championships do not come quickly and there are no short-cuts.

If you want to be a champion in life, then you will puke.

Pandemics, business failures, financial hardships, loss of confidence, depression, social anxiety, medical problems, disease, housing issues, failing, litigation, addiction, writer's block, losses, getting passed over, fired, fear, changing careers, other's criticism of us, moving cities, embarrassment, stress, death of a loved one, injuries, family troubles, and bad performances are just a small sample of how we all puke.

Fear of these events occurring and experiencing hardships, difficulties, frustrations, break-ups, and breakdowns are sadly what prevent some people from attempting the difficult paths of life.

Trying to accomplish something that you've never done means that you'll encounter so much resistance and suffering and setbacks that only those who can truly endure will make it.

Because of the difficulty of the journey and the challenges and struggle that await us, many people try to avoid puking. They simply do not sign up for the race or contest, nor enter life. They stand on the sidelines. They play it safe.

There appears to be no risk, no failure, and no puking involved when on the sidelines. But *nothing* can prevent puking. We have all puked. There is no reward for playing it safe in life.

The sideline life simply causes a different kind of suffering, and it's a slow decay. It becomes just a different kind of struggle. There are major downsides with no reward, little meaning, excitement, or impact. People become isolated, lack connection in relationships, and become absent of an overall purpose. Negativity, complacency, and depression are some of the evils that infect these people.

The purpose of life is to have a purpose.

Life is not a spectator sport! It requires courage.

If you've played this video game called *life*, there will be many levels and reset buttons along the way. No gamer conquers all the levels at once. They take many hours with many setbacks, figuring out what works and what doesn't in order to advance.

Courage can't be found underneath your couch. It is not something that is achieved watching TV or on your phone. It has to be encountered in the world.

Courage is an experience. But it is not a one-time event. Courage only results from a series of setbacks and failures.

We will make repeated mistakes, over and over again. We will fail. Only when we continue to move forward, refusing to give up, do we begin to exercise courage and rally.

While we all will puke in some area of life, we will not all rally.

Rallying becomes a choice; it takes mental toughness.

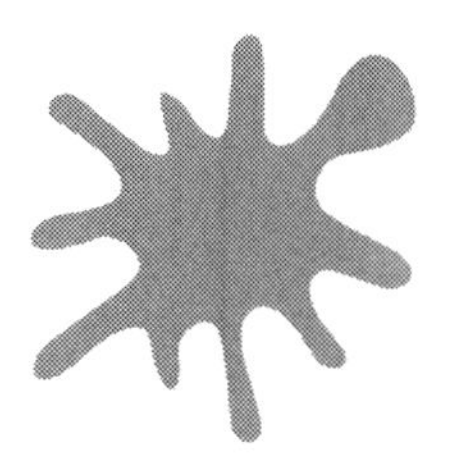

LIFE IS NOT A MARATHON

> *"Mankind can only enjoy that which is achieved through hard work and toil. The harder you work for something, the more you enjoy it. The hard is what makes it great."*—Barkley Marathoner

LIFE IS AN endurance race.

People tout, *"Life is a marathon, not a sprint."* Well, it's closer to a 100-mile hilly trail run, rather than a 26.2-mile flat road race. Life is harder and more complicated than we think it is.

However, we all have to run our own race. And every one of our journeys and passions and contributions will vary.

Personally, I love endurance races and the challenge of doing things that are extremely tough. I also need the discipline and outlet that the training provides. The skill of endurance transfers into real life.

The huge impact of endurance races, however, is the community.

Races in general are made special because of the people involved. Any event that brings out the best in one another creates a bond.

We all become connected through the struggle.

Races where humans cheer on, encourage, and help each other out are the best. It's about giving and receiving the love from fellow competitors and supporters. When you see others suffering alongside, doing the same difficult tasks, it pushes you. The bond is created amongst competitors and everyone involved. It's one reason why we are called the human race.

The best part about life is the community we surround ourselves with. When others are attempting their best, we get to experience the finest side of humanity. It is easiest to care about people when everyone is trying to accomplish the same challenging goal.

It's tough to witness this camaraderie and love for one another in everyday life, sitting in traffic or in the supermarket line, especially in the era of *social distancing*. We have to be in the arena and not on the sidelines of life to witness and experience the community.

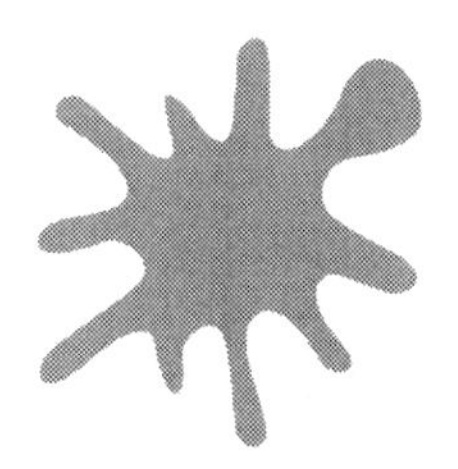

WHY WE PUKE

"What does it take to break you?"—Nick Saban

OUR MIND HAS one role.

Its job is to keep us safe.

That's it. Stay safe.

The mind's primary function is to protect us, which is a survival instinct, and it does an excellent job. It served us well hundreds and thousands of years ago when the immediate threats to our survival were more prominent. Currently, however, most of the threats we face are not as clear.

Our mind does not want us to take risks. It seeks out potential threats and reminds us to avoid them. Feeling fear, nervousness, and anxiousness is our mind's job of keeping us away from any discomfort or harm.

Our mind is simply not interested in our goals or aspirations. It cares nothing about being the best that we can be, or even about getting better.

Its job is to keep us safe!

The challenge is that we compete against our own mind. Sadly, our own mind has a strategic advantage over us.

It knows our strengths and weaknesses. It has advanced knowledge about our triggers and dislikes. It also has an unlimited storage dedicated to our previous failures and setbacks and situations that caused us pain or suffering. So any time we sense discomfort, uneasiness, or potential harm, our mind will shock us into avoiding that situation or fighting our way out of it.

Imagine competing against someone who already knows the moves that you are going to do. Attempting to beat someone who knew everything about you is as tough as it gets.

That's the battle.

Our mind stores these memories to keep us safe the next time we are in the vicinity of a threat. It has clever tactics and strategies to keep us safe. It will tell us lies and half-truths, and rationalize our own actions, just to keep us safe.

Here's how it works.

When we are in situations that cause stress, our arousal level increases. Let's say we are delivering a presentation or giving a speech. We want it to go well, so we'll experience tons of feelings: uneasy stomach, racing thoughts, clammy hands, sweating, and so on. If we face uncertainty about our future because of an event, then we will experience the same protective feelings, we may lose sleep, experience anxiety, and imagine the worst-case scenario. That's how our mind will operate, and it will try to protect us during any times of risk or insecurity.

Our mind wants us to shut it down because it is a threat. Something bad could happen. This is why we are competing against our own mind.

However, we need to override our own mind and perceive the situation as a challenge or an opportunity. We are in a battle over which thoughts can be beneficial to us and which thoughts are intended only to keep us safe.

We have to know which voice to obey in order to trust our own decisions and ourselves.

It's not about the puke.

It's about the rally.

It's not about the setback.

It's about the comeback.

CATASTROPHE

"If you want to understand what wins, you have to understand what loses."—Bill Parcells

JORDAN SPIETH WAS the number one ranked amateur golfer in the world before he was 18 years of age. By this time, he already shared the same sentence as Tiger Woods because they were the only two-time winners of the U.S. Junior Amateur Golf Championship.

He played golf at the University of Texas, winning two tournaments as a freshman. He was voted freshman player of the year and became a first-team All-American. He led the Texas Longhorns team in winning the NCAA championship.

In 2012 he turned professional, and just two weeks before his 20th birthday he was near the lead in the final round of the John Deere Golf Classic. As a harbinger of future finishes, on the very last hole of the tournament, Spieth holed out an amazing bunker shot to join the playoff where he beat Zach Johnson, the defending champion of the event.

With this victory, he became the fourth youngest player to win a PGA Tour event.

Spieth's strength was not always his physical game, like driving distance or accuracy, nor was it his iron-play. His greatest attribute was his mental strength and his ability to putt the ball like a Greek god.

Spieth had the fire and competitiveness needed to be the best in the world, and he also possessed an intangible quality. This intangible was the notion of *another gear*. He possessed the "it" factor referred to in the greatest of athletes. It's almost impossible to gauge, but Michael Jordan and Tiger Woods were also able to raise their games to the level required when it was needed the most. This quality of a champion is always seen in those who rise to the occasion and come through in the greatest moments.

In 2015, Spieth had an epic year as he won a total of five events. He won two PGA Tour events and two majors, including the Masters and U.S. Open. He became the second youngest player ever to win the Masters, and in doing so he tied Tiger Woods scoring record. His fifth victory of the season was The Tour Championship.

He was the PGA Tour player of the year and became the number #1 ranked golfer in the world.

In 2016, Jordan Spieth continued his dominance and won the first PGA tournament of the year, the Tournament of Champions. He won the tournament by 8 shots.

At the Masters in 2016, as the defending champion, he entered the final round with the lead. During the front nine holes at Augusta National, he made four straight birdies with no bogies and extended his lead to five shots.

He had a five shot lead with nine holes to play.

There is a popular saying in golf that the Masters does not actually begin until the back nine on Sunday. Many players throughout history have had difficult finishes to the Masters, which did not allow them to win.

But this situation was different. He had experience and previous success in these situations many times before. He had the best short game in the tournament and was in complete control.

Golf writers had already started penning their narrative, but no one could have predicted what occurred next. Golf is fickle, and even professional players are one shot away from believing that they are the best, but also one shot away from thinking they are the worst.

Jordan Spieth made back-to-back bogies at holes 10 and 11. But he still held a comfortable lead. As he stood on the tee box at the par-three 12th hole, he knew what he wanted and needed to do, which was to hit it on the green.

The 12th hole is the most famous hole at the Masters. Framed pictures adorning walls in people's homes have this hole as the centerpiece. There is a creek in front of the hole and three bunkers surrounding the green that serve as its defense.

During the first three rounds of the tournament, the scoring at the twelfth hole is average. However, during the final round, it becomes one of the toughest scoring holes. It's still a straightforward shot, except the situation, wind, and trouble surrounding the Sunday hole placement make it crucial.

Jordan unfortunately hit a poor shot with his 9-iron and admitted later that he took a quick swing. His ball found the water short of the green.

Since he had a five shot lead starting the back nine, if he could have finished the twelfth hole with a double-bogey, he still would have remained in the lead.

But what sometimes takes place when pressure mounts, a mistake occurs, and people are in the toughest of spots is that additional errors can happen.

Spieth then hit another poor shot, and again landed it in the water. He took a quadruple bogey, seven, on the hole. It was his first quadruple bogey in professional competition.

His mental toughness was still evident and he rebounded and birdied the 13th and 15th holes and still shot two under par for the rest of his round. However, the gap was too much to overcome and he finished second.

So, how did this lapse and ultimate collapse happen to the world's best golfer?

All performers have an optimal range of arousal under pressure. When arousal gets too high, however, it turns into anxiety. The anxiety during a performance can cause some mistakes, but there can be an extreme drop-off in performance or even a *catastrophe.* [1]

Under extreme pressure, with a high reward on the outcome, performance does not follow a path of slow decline or fade. There is an *extreme* drop-off in performance.

The *"catastrophe"* is caused by one error or mistake, which leads to a complete drop-off, meltdown, or collapse.

Just one mistake from the world's greatest athletes in high-pressure situations can cause a collapse. They may start to think too much, focus on the wrong cues, and actually feel the anxiety in their body. It causes them to experience another mistake and another, just like a ball rolling down a hill. It's a negative cycle and happens quickly.

If you have ever taken an important test and were stumped on an early question, it may have caused your anxiety to spike, which led to doubt and a slight panic in your system. The panic at that moment had the potential to cause an extreme drop in your confidence and performance on that test.

It happens in all sports. It occurs in all of life.

A catastrophe is what happened to Jordan Spieth. Here is the best in the world, a future Hall of Fame golfer, one of the most mentally tough performers, and a collapse happened.

It happens to everybody.

Everybody pukes.

In 2009, then Supreme Court Chief Justice John Roberts administered the oath of office to President-elect, Barack Obama.

This historic ceremony had thousands in attendance and millions watching on TV. Chief Justice Roberts decided to memorize the 35 words to the oath instead of reading them. However, he messed up the words. There was a small pause at the beginning of the oath, followed by a huge gaffe with the word order of "faithfully." Obama recognized it, and paused before Chief Justice repeated the words and corrected it.

A huge controversy followed that President Obama wasn't legally President. Thus, just as a precaution, they conducted the oath again the following day.

Here is an intelligent man, in the highest position of the judicial branch, on a historic day in United States history, and he essentially puked in front of millions watching.

What is important to realize and comprehend is that even though he puked, Chief Justice Roberts rallied.

This mistake, an embarrassing moment for the Chief Supreme Court judge, had no bearing on the career and work and decisions that John Roberts made as Chief Justice of the Supreme Court.

Jordan Spieth would also rally.

A LAPSE OR A COLLAPSE?

> *"Many of life's failures are people who did not realize how close they were to success when they gave up."*—Thomas Edison

GORDON ALAN MARLATT was a pioneer in addiction and alcohol dependence research. He led the movement for a new approach towards treatment.

Early research about alcohol abuse focused only on biological factors. However, genetics accounted for only about 50% of alcoholism. The remaining 50% of the risk factors of alcohol abuse or addiction were environmental factors, such as life stress, social support, and repeated exposure to the drug. [2]

In direct contrast to other leading researchers during the 1970s, Marlatt found that exposure to "high-risk situations" led people to relapse. It was how individuals were able to cope with difficult situations that determined the length of sobriety.

Marlatt's research became known as the *Abstinence Violation Effect.* Exposure to a high-risk situation that an alcoholic faced was an initial trigger toward a relapse. Triggers could be numerous: a celebration, being around others who were drinking, or feeling sad and depressed. A *violation* occurred when there was a break in the abstinence. What took place thereafter was the *effect.*

How would people respond to the lapse in sobriety? Would the violation cause someone to return to their old-pattern of drinking and their old ways, or would the violation simply be a one-time lapse?

Having a lapse was a huge indicator of someone returning to a full relapse, but it was not inevitable. Marlatt uncovered that there was a difference between people who had a lapse or slip and those who suffered a relapse or collapse, which was a full return to substance use.

The difference between a lapse and a full collapse was due to one important mental skill. This mental skill is required if we want to rally. It's the same skill used whether winning major championships, staying sober, or sticking to New Year's resolutions.

ABSTINENCE VIOLATION EFFECT

"You have the talent to succeed, but do you have the courage to fail?"—Donita Walters

THE MAJORITY OF New Year's resolutions are to lose weight and/or exercise more. However, the annual failure rate is almost 80%. These numbers stay consistent regardless of what new technology or gadget has been introduced to combat the issues.

Without fail, New Year's resolutions fail.

This negative cycle repeats itself every year. By the second week of February, just six weeks into the New Year, most people have dropped their resolutions.

Even though there are dozens of strategies, hacks, tips, and techniques for keeping New Year's resolutions, the goals still fail. Anyone can Google the answer, so lack of knowledge is not the reason.

The reason these resolutions fail is due to the same factors as why professional athletes sometimes puke under extreme pressure and why alcoholics and addicts have a collapse.

It's the *one mistake.*

Here's how the process happens.

The New Year's resolution or goal began well. The goal was full of promise and optimism because this was a new leaf, a new you. The progress started off solid and you felt proud, in control, and more confident.

Then unfortunately something happened.

Perhaps our kid was sick and we missed our workout. Maybe we just slept in and blew it off. Or even though we swore off deserts, we indulged after dinner and ate that piece of cake.

However it happened, we messed up.
Life happens.
Mistakes happen.
We puke.
We had a setback.

It isn't the fall from grace, it's the fall OUT from grace that causes the complete collapse.

The *one mistake* causes the relapse.

The first workout that we miss or piece of cake that we eat causes an *extreme* drop in our performance.

The reality is that missing one workout, or eating one piece of cake, means little. Just like actually going through one workout won't make any difference physically, messing up once won't make any difference either, physically.

But too often we miss another workout or since we already had that piece of cake, we might as well eat the whole damn cake. All it takes is our poor response to *one mistake* or slip up and the mentality can quickly become "screw it, I blew it."

But, we process the mistake differently. Messing up one time makes us feel like we failed. Our anxiety spikes and now we have to deal with the major setback. We set a goal, an expectation, where *any* slip feels like a failure. We probably weren't aware of it, but perfection was the goal that we had set. We certainly didn't set the goal to fail, knowing or hoping that we wouldn't make it.

The *one mistake* does not cause the collapse. It's our response to the mistake.

The *abstinence violation effect* rings true in all areas of health, wealth, and improvement. Even people with life-threatening diseases allow that one setback to result in a complete collapse.

Approximately 40% of all patients fail to adhere to their treatment plans. Patients often forget, misunderstand, or simply ignore their prescribed treatment regime. [3]

Research was conducted on exercise with individuals with severe Type-2 diabetes. These people's lives depended on getting well. And even though they signed up for the research study, demonstrating that they were motivated, dropout rates still hovered around 50%.

Their one mistake led to a collapse.

Why does one mistake cause a collapse?

FIRST, THE NEGATIVE outweighs the positive.

We remember the one bad experience at a restaurant more than the ten positive ones that we had at the same place. We pay more attention to the few negative reviews on a website than we do the dozens of positive ones.

The negative outweighs the positive because bad news headlines sell more than good news. And the feeling of losing $100 is sometimes more painful than the good feeling of winning $100.

The negative outweighs the positive. It's why we *hate* to lose more than we *love* to win.

Think of negativity like getting a cold. If there are sick people in the same space that we work and play, then the chances increase that more people will catch it. And all it takes is one sick person. If we live or work or play with mostly positive, upbeat, and energetic people, but there still remains a negative influencer, they will get other people sick.

The negative outweighs the positive when it comes to our own mind as well. The months or years of sobriety mean little after a slip or a lapse. Without proper perspective and coaching from others, the lapse leads to a collapse. During an actual performance, one mistake is a shock to our entire system and it forces us to reset.

Since it outweighs the positive, it is far easier to simply be negative than it is to be positive.

It is easier to criticize someone or a situation than it is to compliment them. The leisurely life is more commonly lived than the disciplined day to day. It is more comfortable to not run or workout than it is to get out there and do it (at least for the moment). In the simplest terms, it's easier to do *nothing* than it is to do *something*. And we as individuals always seek the path of least resistance. Our mind wants us to do the least possible work in order to achieve the greatest possible outcome.

We are always fighting the same battles within ourselves. This is a war where we win more battles than we actually lose, but we are reminded of the losses and setbacks more frequently because they are so painful and disparaging.

The trouble is the emotional connection of feeling defeated. It is the negativity that causes us to fall off completely. There is pain and guilt in messing up. It hurts. There is a drastic negative cycle because the negative far outweighs the positive.

There is a saying amongst NFL coaches that when you win you feel good for a day, but when you lose you feel bad for a week.

The emotional connection between our self and self-worth is because of how we perform. When we do well, we feel good, at least for a while. But when we do poorly, or mess up, the negative emotion is stronger and much more impactful.

The powerful negative feelings that we experienced at some point in our lives resurface. For many, these damaging feelings are regret, guilt, and shame.

The emotions, the shame and guilt of messing up, are painful. It often hurts worse than quitting because when we quit, we no longer have to keep returning to the scene of the crime. We can more easily stop going to our workout class than explain why we missed it. It's easier to stop attending classes than it is to keep going and explain our shame or wonder what people think.

But the setback can cause more damage than just our hurt emotions. The fallout from grace causes us to experience the worst of all punishments: A loss of confidence.

No matter how well we have been doing, our confidence is sometimes cut down with one mighty swing of the axe.

One mistake can cause this to happen.

THE FALLOUT OF A SETBACK

"People are lonely because they build walls instead of bridges."—Joseph Newton

THE RESULT OF pain and a setback is the same, isolation.

The setback causes us to isolate. And it starts and continues a vicious negative cycle.

However, isolation and withdrawing oddly becomes what the body starts to crave, even though it's the worst possible solution for us.

When we struggle, our emotional sensitivity is heightened and we feel even more negativity. Exhaustion, fear, guilt, and shame sets in and takes hold. Perhaps we blamed others for our mistake, or we quickly retreated into a state of self-hatred or depression. Due to our isolation, our mood worsens and we feel even more alone.

Isolation means not being able to confide in and connect with others. Shame and guilt from a setback also causes us to keep secrets. There are few people posting updates that they blew their New Year's resolutions *again*. We avoid posting that our loved one's relapsed. We hide our pain and keep secrets.

However, we are only as sick as our secrets.

The fallout of a setback is losing our connection with others and losing confidence in ourselves.

Social isolation is the worst type of punishment. Sometimes, we inflict it upon ourselves.

We are social creatures.

The most dangerous type of incarceration for prisoners is solitary confinement. Numerous studies into the effects of solitary confinement on prisoners have shown serious detriments after just 10 days. Isolation puts prisoners at risk for serious mental illness, and has severe emotional, cognitive, and social consequences. [4]

The results from solitary confinement cause people to become more self-centered, irritable, and defensive. Isolation breeds anxiety, depression, and hopelessness.

Separation puts the brain on high alert and causes people to distort their own minds and their view of others. Instead of viewing social connections as something to be made, the isolated brain instead views most people as threats.

Harry Harlow was an American psychologist who accepted a professorship at the University of Wisconsin. He immediately leapt into his life-long research, which was with primates. His laboratory bred and reared Rhesus monkeys.

His early studies focused on cognition and learning, and he discovered that monkeys were "learning to learn." The studies were innocent enough at the start, and he researched mother-infant bonding. His early experiments were designed to bring *love into the laboratory.*

In 1971, sadly, Harlow's wife died after her several-year bout with cancer. Harlow personally experienced depression and his research reflected it. He became entranced in researching depression and isolation with the monkeys.

In one of his studies, he looked at the effects of separation on baby monkeys and their mothers. The groups of baby monkeys consisted of complete separation from their mothers and placed in total social isolation for various periods of time: 3 months, 6 months, and 1 year.

The results were disturbing, and showed that even at 3 months of isolation, the baby monkeys suffered psychological damage. They had bizarre behavior and struggled at any interaction with other monkeys. The effects of those at 3 months however could be reversed, given time. [5]

It was the effects on the monkeys who were isolated for 1 year without a mother that appeared to be irreversible. When introduced to other monkeys, they barely moved and did not explore or play. Some of the monkeys who had been isolated for over a year even refused to eat.

The monkeys' so-called "basic needs" of food and shelter were met, but the isolation with their mother or others caused extreme maladjustment.

The caregiving of a mother produced a safe and secure bond, which then reflected the baby monkey's view of the outside world. A secure relationship with their mother early on meant the outside world was also the same. The monkeys with the early bond approached the world where other connections could then be made.

However, the lack of connection and bond showed monkeys would have extreme psychological disturbances and would be unable to connect.

His research showed that the bond and connection with others was as important as food to the overall development of a person. Without the connection, the baby rhesus monkeys were unable to make a comeback.

But, while one mistake can cause the *setback*, "it only takes one" for the *comeback*!

THE RALLY

"One opportunity is all you need."—Jesse Owens

EVERY DOOR HAS a hinge.

A door without a hinge is a wall, it just doesn't work. When you hear about doors opening or closing in life, it's because of the hinge. If we ever listen to a rusty door, it's not the door that's rusty at all, it's the hinge.

Small hinges can swing big doors.

The importance is that no matter how bad our situation is or how bleak an outcome appears to be, *IT ONLY TAKES ONE*!

We can't connect the dots moving forward, we can only connect the dots looking backwards. Thus, when we look back in our lives, we will witness that it was one moment that made all the difference. Perhaps it was meeting one person, or making one play, or just one decision.

There will be multiple hinge moments that occur in our lives. But we often can't tell the significance of the moment in the actual moment. Most of the time, it's hours, days, weeks, or months later that we realize the impact that that one moment had on our lives. Or even years.

Some of our hinge moments or people may be born out of extreme hardship and duress. Catastrophes, tragedies, even pandemics are immediate, because from that moment, everything is different. The importance of mental toughness is that we have no idea when or who that hinge is coming!

But, it only takes one!

We are always just one person, one moment, or one decision away from our comeback.

Jordan Spieth had to endure and block out much criticism over the next season about his *not* winning the Masters. When there appears to be a kink in the hose of an athlete, the media pounces all over their fall from grace.

It's crucial to understand the Reggie Jackson quote, *"They don't boo nobodies."* If you do anything worthy or significant, people around you will criticize you. The only way to avoid criticism is by not doing anything at all and stay on the sidelines of life.

Media was simply built on creating storylines and controlling the narrative of *"Would Spieth ever bounce back?"* Imagine that, all of the accomplishments and victories that he had and the negative headlines dominated the narrative.

When the 2017 Open Championship began, at Royal Birkdale, England, Jordan Spieth simply was not really a favorite. However, he played well and even began the final round with a three-shot lead. Unfortunately, as golf can dictate, he started off poorly and made three bogeys in his first four holes. He three-putted the ninth green and his attitude was, *"Hit it close, because my putter was failing me."*

He was still tied for the lead with Matt Kuchar on the 13th hole when another hinge moment occurred. Spieth hit his tee shot way right, over the fans, barely on the property!

Media quickly hopped on the theme that Spieth would repeat his unsuccessful performance at the Masters. Spieth had also grown tired from that narrative and used it instead to motivate himself after his wayward tee shot.

How the sequence of events unfolded was natural drama at its finest.

He had to take an unplayable lie, which not only cost him a shot but he was forced to take a drop before hitting his next shot. However, due to his position on the course, there was no good spot to drop the ball.

The cameras were showing exactly where he was on the course along with the rules officials discussing where he could drop. He was so far off line that he was literally next to all of the support trailers and the driving range.

It took him and his caddie, Michael Greller, almost 15 minutes before Spieth even attempted his next shot. After the deliberation, in a highly stressful environment, he hit his shot just short of the green and made an 8-footer to *save bogey*. Some bogeys are better than others in the difficult sport of golf, and this one was remarkable after everything that had transpired.

This setback served as the catalyst for the rest of his round.

Jordan Spieth proceeded to go *birdie-eagle-birdie-birdie* over the next four holes to win the British Open by three-shots. It was simply amazing and one of the best finishes in any Major championship.

He became the youngest American to win the Open Championship.

The calamity and suffering and puking that occurred at the Masters the year prior prepared him for the comeback to hold up the Claret Jug trophy.

It only takes one!

Puke
&
Rally.

Rally *(Verb)*

A mustering of scattered forces to renew an effort. A summoning up of strength or courage after weakness or dejection. A renewed offensive.

A rally is a good thing. It is inherent of overcoming some sort of adversity. Mustering, summoning, and renewing are the enticing actions needed to rally.

Puking is not an option; we are all going to puke. It is not pleasant.

Rallying, however, often is a choice.

The interesting part about the rally is that it involves other people. A rally in tennis, teams that rally, or even a campaign rally, all involve other people.

Jordan Spieth displayed the impressive mental skill of confidence in his comeback. Gordon Marlatt also found confidence to be the differentiator in alcoholics. Confidence was one variable that ultimately determined an alcoholic's precious sobriety.

Nothing can prevent a setback, but confidence and connection determines our own comeback. The same mental skill applies to how we cope when life delivers us a setback.

We know that failure is inevitable and will occur.

However, puking is an event, it's not a person!

Failure is a bruise, not a tattoo.

If we are unable to move past our mistakes, bruises, lapses, slumps, lulls, defeats, and setbacks, then we will be unable to have a comeback. Life is the same way; we need to be able to move on from the mistakes, the slips, and the errors that we have made.

We have to let *it* go, learning from the painful event. Once we let go of it, it lets go of us.

Show me someone who can let go of mistakes, and I'll show you somebody who is primed for a comeback.

Letting go and refocusing after mistakes is a talent, and some will do it better than others. However, those who can refocus actually display the mental skill of confidence.

Confidence and connection is how we rally!
Confidence is simply the belief that it will all work out.

We don't know how it will work out, and that's what causes us stress and anxiety, but that's also why it's called belief. Faith is sometimes only really faith until it's all you've got.

Confidence is contagious because it affects all of our other mental skills.

We can only refocus and let go of mistakes *if* we are confident that we can come back. Letting go of failure can only be accomplished *if* we believe and have confidence that the result will eventually turn out for the better. If you show me someone who can let go of mistakes, I'll show you someone who is confident.

The mental skill of confidence also impacts our motivation. When we are confident, we are more motivated and determined. If we know that we are going to achieve a certain result then we are all-in with working as hard as we can. If we know the outcome will work out then we know we just have to keep pushing through the difficult times. Even though we don't know when the positive outcome will happen, *if* we believe that it will, we become just that much more inspired as a result.

When we are confident, we are more patient and forgiving. If we know that we will rally and have a comeback, it provides us major leeway in how we treat others and ourselves. We let go of mistakes easier when we possess a lot of confidence. Confidence changes our thought process from our setbacks being a tattoo into just being a bruise.

Confidence is the elixir.
Confidence is king.

In the game of chess, when the king dies, the game is over! If there is a loss of confidence and belief, it's tough to get it back. We have to start a new game.

Confidence can be lost when we have the one mistake, the missed workout, or the error. In our lives, when we have been shattered and are feeling lost and broken, it can take a while to get back on track.

So, how do we build and re-build our confidence to overcome the setback?

THE RECIPE FOR A COMEBACK

HAVING PURPOSE IN THE SETBACK

"Fear takes us further than we want to go and keeps us longer than we want to stay." —Anonymous

WHEN YOU'RE SUFFERING or experiencing a setback in life, there needs to be purpose. Finding meaning in your setback means having the courage to go past your current limits, your excuses, your thresholds, and discover who you currently are and who you want to become.

There is also an angle about suffering that brings perspective and gratitude back to life. It is part of our human nature to take things for granted. We all do it. We lose gratitude, thankfulness, and perspective.

Once we go through difficult times and situations, rest and recovery take on new meaning. Simple things in life have new appreciation after doing tough stuff. For instance, running 20 miles involves a bit of suffering, which in turn makes the cup of coffee or stack of pancakes simply taste that much better.

It's only after we've suffered and endured through adversity that we can appreciate the beauty and sanctity of life. People who are truly alive and do cool stuff have overcome and endured the toughest of times.

Victor Frankl was born in 1905 in Vienna, Austria into a Jewish family. The meaning of life intrigued him ever since he was a small child. He was fascinated by the study of psychology and earned his doctorate in medicine in 1925 from the University of Vienna. His specialty was neurology and psychiatry and he was well known in the country.

In 1938, the country of Austria came under German rule, immediately before the onset of WWII. Thousands of Jewish citizens were arrested and deported to concentration camps. Due to his standing in society, he was not immediately arrested, and even married his sweetheart in 1941. However, in 1942, he, his wife, and his parents were deported by the Nazi-led German state.

He was a prisoner in three different concentration camps during WWII.

His wife was killed in the camps and his manuscript, a lifetime of work, was discovered years into his containment and destroyed. He had to recreate his experiences and write it down on stolen pieces of paper.

He, along with millions of others, suffered severe atrocities in the concentration camps. Starvation, beatings, humiliation, and disease were customary for all prisoners. He said that it is incomprehensible for those outside to truly understand how little life was valued in those camps. Except that it *"tore open the human soul and exposed its depths."*[6]

The rate of survival for prisoners was 1 in 28.

Victor Frankl ultimately published the exceptional book, *Man's Search for Meaning.*

He focused on how we find meaning in our lives. He wrote that even through the worst of conditions and ultimate suffering, we still possessed a small amount of freedom. That freedom was that we could still choose how we would react to any negative situation. We were in control of our attitude.

He spoke that life was not meant to be seeking pleasure or avoiding pain, but to have meaning. Our suffering must have meaning to it.

Despite the harshest of external conditions, we could look inward and find our purpose. If we could accept that suffering was part of our fate, we could find our intention.

He wrote that those living in the concentration camps who had lost hope and belief of a near or distant future soon perished. If life became meaningless, the harsh circumstances would soon overtake them.

Frankl merely acknowledged that the difficult situation we are going through has meaning. He advocated that life depended not so much on the product or the outcome, but rather on the process and the journey.

> *"Has all this suffering, all this dying around us, a meaning? For a life whose meaning depends on such a happenstance—as whether one escapes or not—ultimately would not be worth living at all."*[6]

Many prisoners asked the question, *"Will I survive the camp?"* Survival and escaping was a very important question and a goal for all of them. Wouldn't you ask that question as well, *"Will I survive?"*

The prisoners placed the meaning of their lives *only* in an outcome. However, Frankl reversed it by saying that if their current suffering did not produce meaning, there would be little meaning to survival.

Frankl spoke to the process of finding meaning in the setback as being more important than actual survival. Frankl changed the focus from the outcome and escaping to discovering purpose inside of the suffering.

The reason why Victor Frankl uncovered the truth about the human spirit was through his connection with others. The shared experience with other prisoners allowed him to witness raw human beliefs and actions. It was through this experience that he developed enough confidence in his own work to share it and help others.

We build our confidence through our connection with others.

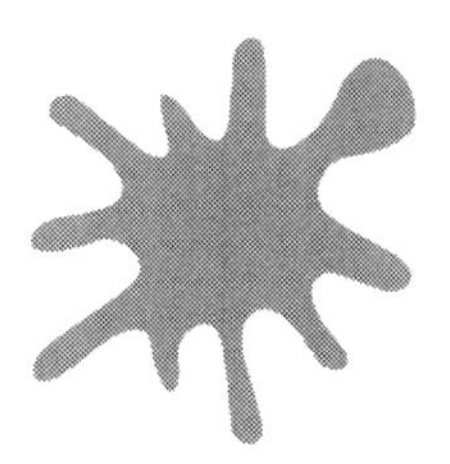

CONNECTION

"Setbacks are awful tasting medicine, but just what the patient needs."—Steve Jobs

JORDAN SPIETH OFTEN referred to his successful rounds of golf and wins as "we." It was a team effort and the connection with his caddie, Michael Greller, helped propel him to his comeback. Especially during the Open Championship, Greller instilled calmness when needed and helped provide Jordan with confidence. After his Open Championship win, Spieth stated, *"This is as much his as it is mine."*

The opposite of isolation is connection.

Connection with others is how we build our confidence. It is what provides us purpose in our setback. Through our connections with others is how we come back.

Connection is how we build confidence.

However, we lack connection and as a result we lack confidence.

- Almost 50% of Americans are lonely.
- In the United Kingdom, nine million people, almost 1/5th of the population, are reported to be lonely.
- 40,000 people in Japan die from loneliness every year. [7]

Instead, what we have in life is contact. *Contaction* is not a typo. It is an obsolete term noted most recently as 1913. Probably won't get away with it in a game of *Words with Friends* or *Scrabble,* though.

Contaction means "an act of touching."

We look at our phones and touch our devices almost every 12 minutes, which is about 80 times a day. We have an unlimited amount of contact with people and events and information.

But, there is little deep connection.

Even though we are "connected" to the broader world through these social outlets, it's an illusion of understanding and empathy. Indeed, more contact takes place in the day-to-day on-goings of people, but the depth of connection is far apart.

Connection is *meaningful quality...*
Contaction is *meaningless quantity...*

We can get likes from others, post our own highlight reels, and in turn like others' posts. It provides an instant rush of dopamine. That's fine, but it can leave us unfulfilled, because it's a transaction behind a screen, not a transformation face to face.

Connection is more important than contaction. Connection goes beyond contact. Connection builds our confidence.

The difficult part, however, is actually connecting with others.

We possess in our DNA a longing to feel included and part of something special. Connection with friends, loved ones, organizations, teams, or even causes larger than ourselves. Only when we feel an emotional connection does our life begin to reach its potential.

Connections and feelings of belonging provide individuals with a shared sense of self, stability in their identity, and allow each other to pursue higher goals.

An event, occasion, or celebration can brings us together, but can it hold us in place?

Think about the strongest bonds that you've had with one another. Did you live in a same-shared environment, like a class or office space? Were you connected through a team? Did your relationship consist of a shared belief system when you saw each other in church? Was fitness and belonging to the same gym your connection? Perhaps your kids were on the same soccer team, or you lived in the same neighborhood.

How we become and stay connected has a major impact on the potential depth of our relationships. The best relationships are not one-dimensional.

The potential connection exists with others merely because of our contact with others. However, this contact sometimes leads to life-altering connections.

THE LIGHTNING CONNECTION

"Rainbows are visions, they're only illusions, and rainbows have nothing to hide."—Kermit the Frog

THE RAINBOW CONNECTION is a great song. It's a song symbolic of hope. While rainbows are real, they aren't actually there. You can't touch them.

Lightning on the other hand is real and it delivers a potent connection.

It is the most powerful force that one can imagine and it directly connects the atmosphere with the earth.

Lightning strikes can have temperatures of 20,000 degrees Celsius, which is hotter than the sun. It can produce up to 10 billion watts of power. Meaning, just one strike could power up to 56 homes for an entire day.

It is fast and the strokes travel at speeds of 220,000 miles per hour, which is approximately one-third the speed of light. Compare that to the speed of thunder, which is about 750 miles per hour. [8]

It is estimated that there are over 100,000 thunderstorms per year, producing over 25 million lightning strikes. That's an average of more than a hundred lightning bolts every second across the globe.

Lightning needs a cloud.

Hot air rises and water vapor cools to form a cloud. The cloud then grows larger, turning the water vapor into ice. These ice particles move around, crashing into one another and creating an electrical charge—lightning.

Clouds have a concentrated negative charge and the earth has a positive charge. The positive charge from the ground *contacts* with the negative charge from the clouds and the spark of lightning connects.

There are many factors for lightning to contact the ground: prevailing winds, time of the year, altitude, temperature, and humidity are the most common.

This normal "negative" lightning from cloud to ground occurs in about 95% of all strikes.

But there is an even more dangerous and powerful type of lightning.

The most destructive lightning initiates from the top of the cloud as opposed to the bottom, and because of the distance it must travel to the ground, its electromagnetic field is that much stronger.

This type of lightning is aptly labeled *positive lightning.*

Because of the greater charge, the strike lasts longer than a typical bolt of lightning and can be as much as 10 times more powerful. It can even travel up to 20 miles! It is the cause of most forest fires and lethal strikes in people. [9]

This is the lightning that comes from *"out of the blue."*

Since positive lightning is far rarer and accounts for only about 5% of all strikes, the scientific community knows far less about this type of lightning.

Lightning is the atmosphere's contact with earth, but it also serves as a connection. For instance, the largest wild fires are caused by lightning strikes and because they go undetected for a longer time, they become the largest burns.

Wildfires, although destructive to man, are essential to the overall growth and health of forests. They clean up debris on the forest floor, provide needed nutrients to the soil, and kill off insects that destroy vegetation.

These lessons and reminders about lightning are nice. But the same important lightning that occurs in the atmosphere and connects to the earth is exactly what occurs with people as well.

The positive lightning that transforms forests through wildfires is the same phenomenon that occurs within us. Those who are struck by positive lightning receive a transformation.

We need connection.

Lightning Connections in us

"The same lightning that causes forest fires also fertilizes the plants."—Anonymous

Just as storms emerge in the atmosphere, storms brew inside of people as well. Storms form when we have pain and suffer. These could be feelings of disappointment or fear, we experience rejection or become hungry, angry, lonely, or tired.

Most of us do not handle the internal storms very well. If we do not transform our pain then we will transmit it. Sadly, hurt people hurt other people. The transmission of someone's disappointment takes place in the form of a lightning strike.

Lightning is what happens when a negative charge from someone interacts with someone else. It is powerful and it is fast.

Just like actual lightning, human lightning strikes follow the path of least resistance. Those who are closest to the storm in proximity and relationship will often witness and receive the strike. It is why people who are closest to the storm will experience the lightning strikes the most often. When we are connected with people on a continual basis, such as our family, team, or coworkers, we usually feel any lightning that occurs.

Lightning can strike from anyone if we are within range. It seems with everyone supposedly connected via online, most of us are within range. Most lightning is negatively charged. These strikes can be mild, like someone laughing at us, or they can be severe, like a rumor or even abuse.

However, the most powerful type of lightning can come from *"out of the blue"*, when we least expect it.

It's the positive lightning.

Positive lightning stems from people who we look upon as positive or influential. Maybe it's a coach, parent, teacher, boss, mentor, or someone we look up to. It's the people we generally have a favorable outlook on or whose opinion matters to us.

Positive lightning is a negative comment, criticism, sharp blow, or a feeling of embarrassment.

It's being told *"you're not good enough"* or that *"you can't do something."*

Positive lightning starts fires. The lightning can cause serious damage or it can serve as the variable that determines the path of your entire life.

The setback that will occur in your life will often result in the form of a positive lightning strike, coming from a person you admire and who tries to inform you, *"You can't do it."* It will be fast, powerful, and probably cause an extreme amount of pain. It will trigger doubt and indecision and make you question your goals and passions.

But, just as the forest is transformed from the fire caused by a lightning strike, we need it as well.

It is necessary to have these positive lightning strikes!

It is a hinge moment of connection between who we are and who we will become.

Puke
&
Rally.

Lindsey Stirling grew up in Arizona with parents who told her that they could only afford lessons either for violin or dance, but not both. Even though she liked to dance, she chose violin. So she began taking lessons at five years old.

In fact, her parents only could afford half-lessons once a week, and they were told by an instructor that she couldn't learn how to play in just 15 minutes a week.

However, what she possessed was a passion for playing and performing. Her dad would search the newspapers for any free concerts and performances in the city, and they would go watch as a family.

She progressed.

She loved to dance as well, so as she grew, she combined violin and dance and developed into her true self. Her "true self" would be a theme that would serve her during the most difficult of times of her life.

After years of playing classical music, she was burned out. Thus she found and combined her playing and dance with hip-hop. She entered the world of electronic dance music. She did it not as a way of becoming successful but as way of simply reigniting her passion.

In 2010 she won an audition to be on the fifth season of *America's Got Talent*. She advanced and earned a spot as one of the 68 quarterfinalists on the show. The quarterfinalist episodes were split into acts of twelve and she appeared on the August 3rd show.

The three judges were Piers Morgan, Sharon Osborne, and Howie Mandel.

She was introduced as a "hip-hop violinist."

She was confident as her set began in the quarterfinal round and felt this would be a wonderful performance. As approximately 11.4 million viewers watched, however, it did not go as planned.

About a minute into her performance, Piers Morgan buzzed her with an "X." She completed her set and then received the judges' critiques. Little could she have known that what happened next would change the trajectory of her life.

Piers Morgan was the first to comment and defended his buzzer against Lindsey. He stated his approval, how he really liked combining a traditional instrument and her non-traditional hip-hop style and approach.

Then, lightning struck from "out of the blue." *"I love you and your look, but there was one problem, the violin… There were times when it was okay and then at times it sounded like rats being strangled, that bad."* [10]

Sharon Osborne added her own fodder, *"You're not untalented, but you're not good enough."*

Howie Mandel simply agreed, *"I have to agree with Piers on this one."*

Lindsey Stirling not only didn't advance on *America's Got Talent*, she was crushed!

"[You] go from feeling like you're a million bucks," Stirling stated, *"to the very next day feeling like, 'Wow, no one cares.'"* [10]

After crying in the dressing room, she said feeling embarrassed was an "understatement."

How would you feel if you puked in public?

It was a hinge moment for Lindsey Stirling.

She was told that she was *not good enough* in front of millions of people. She even continued to hear from others outside of the show that her work as a dancing violinist was unmarketable.

But she made a commitment to "prove him wrong." Piers' words on national television galvanized her and made her even more determined.

> *"I feel like I owe a lot to Piers Morgan! He gave me a reason to fight. After I had a good cry and pulled myself up by my bootstraps, that hurt and embarrassment turned into extreme motivation—I'm gonna prove them wrong!"* [11]

Lindsey stayed true to herself and that recipe made all the difference. It meant going against the negativity and other people's opinions. It was a process that she had to go through.

She connected with a cinematographer, David Graham, and released a video titled "Spontaneous me" for her YouTube channel.

She started to move the popularity needle and her recognition and music soared. Her debut album was a massive accomplishment, going platinum certified, and she not only collaborated with other top acts but her next song, *"Crystallize"*, was also a major success.

Her next album and title song was *"Shatter me."* It was symbolic of breaking free of the limitations that we place on ourselves. The day of the single's release, it received 1.3 million views. Her videos to date have received over 5 ½ billion views and she has become one the highest paid female Youtube® stars.

> *"It took me years to realize that they weren't necessarily wrong... they were right. I hadn't earned or developed the skills to be able to dance, to be thrown around up in the air while playing the violin. It's really difficult."* [12]

THE HOT WATER

"Being determined in the face of obstacles is vital."—Dr. Seuss

THE SAME HOT water that softens a potato can also harden an egg. The water is exactly the same, but the effect on that object is different.

The hot water represents the setback.

It is the lightning strike of being told by someone that *"you can't do it"* or "*you're not good enough*." The hot water can also be our current situation or circumstance that shows us we are not good enough.

The tealeaf exposed to hot water, however, does something entirely different than a potato or an egg. The tea changes the entire situation and makes the water something greater.

However, we have no idea how strong a tea bag is until it is placed in boiling water.

We need the hot water!

We need the positive lightning strike!
We need the setback!

There has not been *anyone* that has reached a level of success and significance who has not been told or shown that *"you can't do it"* or *"you're not good enough."*

For most, being told or shown that **you're not good enough** can crush one's dreams and aspirations. However, for the successful, it is what springs them forward to succeed.

It isn't about overcoming the objections that occur, it's actually the opposite. In order to achieve our full potential, being told or shown that you're not good enough is a *required* ingredient to achieving success.

The impact is so powerful that it is essential for success!

It is needed because only after we are in hot water can we witness how strong we really are. It becomes an either/or moment, an absolute.

We can hear those negative words from others and believe them, *or* we can hear those words and believe in ourselves.

We agree with the criticism *or* we agree with ourselves.

We *either* believe the setback *or* we believe in ourselves. The setback becomes a Hinge moment that connects who we are with who we will become.

When Kalin was born, in Arkansas, his mom knew something was wrong. By the age of six months, Sonja Bennett realized that he was not focusing at all on her or even making any noises. Doctors told her that *boys just take longer than girls* to develop.

But mothers have a powerful instinct. And at nine months of age, he was finally diagnosed with autism. And with the autism diagnosis, it was suggested by a therapist that he would never walk or even talk.

Early on in Kalin's life, the projection was true. He didn't sit up until two years old, nor walk until he was four, and was non-verbal until he was seven years of age. Kalin was on the spectrum to be one of the estimated 25-50 percent of kids with autism that remain non-verbal all their lives.

After the early diagnosis, his mother self-proclaimed that she *"went to work."* Even though she consistently read to him and played music for him to encourage his non-verbal skills, it was not until he was eight years old that he was able to hold a conversation. He admitted, *"I was always in a corner, not speaking to anyone, always alone."* [13]

What took place in the 3rd grade became a hinge moment for Kalin and his family. There was a pep rally for the school basketball team, and afterwards Kalin went home and told his dad he wanted to play basketball.

His mother claimed, *"That's when the light came on."* He joined a team, and his self-esteem grew as he learned about teamwork and brotherhood from the sport.

He also grew! By the time he graduated high school, Kalin was 6'10" and weighed close to 300lbs. He went from being told that he'd never walk, to being able to dunk a basketball. He became the first autistic person to sign a Division I scholarship for basketball at Kent State University, Ohio (Kent State has one of the best programs for supporting those with autism).

When asked whether she ever imagined that her son would be this successful, Sonja Bennett said, *"Yes—even when he didn't."* Just like so many amazing mothers are for their children, Sonja Bennett's vision, sacrifice, and determination paved the way to overcoming the odds.

The interesting twist is that Kalin spoke to the therapist who gave him the diagnosis that he might never talk or walk.

He told her, *"I hope you haven't told anybody else that because you could ruin their lives."* [13] As a kid, Kalin did not hear the initial diagnosis but his mother did. It was the therapist's words that helped Sonja Bennett *"get to work."*

Being told her son would never walk or talk was the lightning strike to prove them wrong, and she became the lightning rod.

How many people have received a diagnosis from physicians or experts that were wrong? Their speculation wasn't necessarily incorrect, it was just incomplete. No one can accurately predict the strength of one's soul, or confidence, or determination. They base their decisions on the information of the moment and hence we do the same with that information.

We use it as proof that we are good enough and will come back, or we use it as proof that we will not.

Motivation is often like a torpedo; it is shot looking for a target and something to lock on to. The target could be a goal, a dream, or a mountaintop. The target can also be someone else.

Proving people wrong is a torpedo. It electrifies our own desire and the "haters" become a target. This outwardly driven, proving people wrong mentality works, at least for a while.

It is effective because the negative energy is more powerful than the positive. There is no doubt that it drives us in the short-term. The emotional stir from proving people wrong means having to think about your target, the negative person, and using them as your fuel.

But, it is not sustainable.

Hate has to think. Love does not.

We have to conjure up and think about what the negative people said or how they made us feel. When proving people wrong is our only fuel, it needs more and more of it to produce the same result.

The real danger of proving people wrong is that there is often no turn-off switch. When our energy is directed externally toward the negativity, the torpedo starts looking for other targets. If there is no immediate target, then the anger can turn inward and soon it affects our own mindset and those close to us.

Anger directed outwards equals focus; however, anger directed inward equals depression.

Steve Smith was a five-time NFL pro-bowler and future Hall of Fame wide receiver. He was a small receiver who excelled at imposing his will on his opponents. He played angry. Even though he had a lot of success on the field, he did not have a lot of joy. He created a habit of isolating himself.

He talked trash and was brash, and that was his mentality on the field, but off the field he struggled. His constant self-criticism and inability to let go of mistakes haunted him.

He tore his Achilles tendon midway through what was then supposed to be his final season. At that point in his career, he was just 49 catches away from 1,000 total receptions. Yet while sitting in the hospital room, he ruminated over all of the drops he had had over his ten-year career.

It was only after his career had ended that Steve Smith could speak openly about his self-criticism and bouts of depression.

Tenacity is more important than talent.

When there is a lightning strike and we are shown or told we can't do something, *proving people wrong* goes beyond just the mental skill of motivation. Also, is there a better way to approach proving people wrong?

Boston Scott was a diminutive running back. At 5'7 and 180 lbs in high school, he didn't even start on his high-school football team until his senior year. Whereas players are ranked according to stars, he had zero stars as a recruit and hence received no offers to play football in college.

He enrolled in college just as a student and fall football camp had already begun when a couple of running backs became injured. The head coach tracked him down and he joined the team as a walk-on.

In his senior year in college he was still not listed as a starting player, but he played well and by the end of the season he had earned a starting role. He was fast, so the Saints drafted him in the 6th round. He made the team, but was cut soon afterwards and he joined the practice squad.

To make an NFL roster, by itself, still would have been a success story.

However, he was traded to the Philadelphia Eagles, but was cut during training camp and again relegated to the practice squad.

He was behind four other running backs on the depth chart to start the season. However, injuries decimated the Eagles running backs that season and he started his first NFL game on October 11th, 2019.

Just a few weeks later, he became the NFC offensive player of the week. He scored three rushing touchdowns against the New York Giants in the second half and became the first Eagle since 1945 to achieve that feat.

Boston Scott had a ton of doubters and naysayers and negativity surrounding him his entire life. He had heard it all.

Instead of proving people wrong however, Boston Scott described it as proving the people closest to you *right.* He was so adamant about that type of focus and tenacity because the negative people go away. When you reach a level of success, the doubters from the beginning are no longer there. New haters have replaced them. [14]

However, the people closest to you will remain, through the good and the bad. They will walk with you through the valleys and on the climb, but they will also celebrate with you during the successes.

The comeback has to do with our connection to others.

A campfire starts with a spark.

The sparks lights the *tinder,* which could be a leaf, cotton, paper, anything small to get the spark going. Then the tinder sets the *kindling* on fire, which is the bark, or small twigs, basically anything bigger than the tinder. The tinder lights the kindling and the kindling then lights the *timber.* The timber (or firewood) then really gets the fire going.

If you've ever tried to light a campfire using the essentials (spark, tinder, kindling, and timber), it is difficult. It sounds easy, but everything is easier said than done. Besides, when it's all said and done, more is said than done.

What most people do (me included) is take a short-cut route and fast track it towards starting the fire. We use lighter fluid!

Dosing the tinder and kindling with lighter fluid really gets it going.

Proving people wrong is exactly like using lighter fluid or a fire-starter. It is effective. But, it is also temporary. We can't keep dosing the small fire with fluid and get it to burn continuously. We would have to keep adding it and adding it.

Proving people wrong in life means using the immediate short-term emotional-filled moment to drive and push you. We need to keep remembering the lightning strike, the negative person, the hurtful situation, and it moves us in a specific direction. It's successful, but it's not sustainable.

The focus inside of us will only last depending upon the structure of the fire itself.

The foundation of the campfire is what sustains the heat and warmth and utility. The campfire itself is *proving people right.* Often, we are trying to prove ourselves right! There cannot be a greater fire in life than trying to show ourselves that we can do it.

Are we building the fire to prove everyone wrong that we can do it, or are we building the fire for those closest to us to use the warmth as well? When we are successful, we get to enjoy it ourselves. It means sustaining the fire for everyone.

OVERCOME OR COMEBACK?

Comeback (Noun)

To recover from a deficit in a contest or competition [or life].

SOME BELIEVE THAT you have to have a level of success if you want to experience a comeback. They suggest that if you do not have outward success, then it's not really a comeback, but just overcoming.

I got off the narrow path in high school. My goal was to play baseball in college. But along the way I got caught up in having a "good time." I drank and got high and thought I could still function at a high level. My performance suffered, and when I arrived at college I had a hinge moment.

I fell off an 80-foot cliff.

I was severely injured and should have died. But, I was no longer going to play sports at the collegiate level. I did not know about mental toughness, grit, or resiliency, and since I was in a lot of emotional pain and felt like a failure, I continued to drink.

On April 20th of my freshman year I was involved in a drunk-driving accident. I thankfully was the only one injured, but it was rock bottom. I was embarrassed, devastated, and felt like a fraud and a failure. It was a major setback, and while the pain goes away, the scars from messing up remain.

I had reached a level of internal success and self-belief, but it all came crashing down. It took many years to come back. Sometimes quickly and sometimes slowly, but our comeback will present itself if we keep working for it.

The point is: making mistakes or being told that you are not good enough, either through others' words or your circumstances, is a setback. It's a setback to our attitude and belief about ourselves. Once you have encountered the *setback*, it is now considered a *comeback*.

Yes, you have to overcome in order to have a comeback, which is the point. We have all been told or shown that we are not good enough, so we all can have a comeback. It is up to you. But here you'll see both types of comebacks, people who had outwardly success early and those who had success later.

- This girl was born prematurely in 1940 and was the 20th of 22 children born to her dad that consisted of two marriages. She had double pneumonia, scarlet fever, and polio as a kid. She had such problems with her left leg that she wore a brace from age five to 12. She also was black and grew up in the segregated south. Wilma Rudolph ended up winning three gold medals in the 1960 Olympics. She became one of the first national role models for female and black athletes. Her advocacy transcended sports and opened up avenues for strength and prosperity for marginalized groups within the United States.

- This small horse was described early on as undersized, knobby kneed, and prone to sleeping and eating for long periods of time. He was the butt of stable jokes and called *"lazy"* by his initial trainer. He failed to win any of his first 17 races, and only won ten of his first forty races. Seabiscuit's comeback, however, included being voted horse of the year in 1938. Seabiscuit also beat the reigning triple-crown winner, War Admiral, in a head-to- head race by 4 lengths. He was voted 25th best racehorse of all-time.

- Lebron James, one of the greatest basketball players of all time, was born when his mother was just 16 years old. She raised him single handedly from the age of 19 and had to move 12 times within just three years.

- Simone Biles is one of the most decorated US gymnasts in history. Her mother struggled with substance abuse and her grandparents adopted her.

- J. K. Rowling's manuscript of *Harry Potter and the Sorcerer's Stone* was rejected 12 times and she was told *"not to quit her day job."* To illustrate her character along with her comeback and because she donated so much money to charitable organizations, she dropped off the U.K.'s billionaire list.

- Paul Owen grew up on food stamps and welfare. His father died when he was five years old and his mother died when he was thirteen. He moved around among three states and seven foster homes. Paul eventually earned his PhD, became a published author, and a tenured professor at Montreat College in North Carolina.

- This 17-year old moved to New York City with only $8 dollars in his pocket and a guitar. After a year of playing, while living off others to get away from the cold and hardships, he moved back to Los Angeles. He continued to play, but had a four dollar-an-hour job at a video store and lived in a shack. In 1993, Beck released the song, "Loser," which reached the top 10 in the charts. His first album was released a year later and he has since become a four time platinum-selling musician.

- Tom Brady, the greatest quarterback in the history of the NFL, was the very last player picked in the 2000 NFL draft. There were six other quarterbacks drafted before him. It's tough enough being the last player picked on the schoolyard games!

- Peyton Manning, Hall of Famer and two-time winning Super Bowl quarterback, was always plagued with the moniker of *"can't win the big game."*

- Best-selling author, Stephen King, worked at a laundry and his first novel, Carrie, was rejected 30 times. He threw it in the trash, but his wife fished it out and he submitted it once more. It was finally accepted.

- Dubbed, the "Queen of all-media", Oprah Winfrey was born into extreme poverty in rural Mississippi. She had to wear clothes made out of potato sacks. She was molested and raped as a young girl on different occasions by three different family members. She was pregnant at the age of 14 and her son was born prematurely and died.

- Publishers rejected Dr. Seuss' first book 27 times before *And to think I saw it on mulberry street* was published.

- David Blaine, one of the greatest magicians, once held his breath underwater for over 17 minutes. However, he was born with asthma and a severe leg condition that caused his feet to turn inward. It was because of his setbacks that he was forced to hold his breath as a kid and as a result, he improved dramatically.

- After becoming the youngest governor in California history at age 36 in 1974, Jerry Brown lost three bids at President of the United States. He ended up becoming the oldest governor in California history with his election in 2011.

- Billy Mills won the Olympic Gold Medal in the 10,000 meters and was the last Unites States male runner to do so. Before the Olympics, he needed a new pair of running shoes and was told *"no, we only have shoes for potential medalists."* He ran almost an entire minute faster than he had previously to win.

- Kate DiCamillo clocked up a staggering 473 rejection letters within six years before striking a publishing deal for her first novel, *Because of Winn-Dixie,* which became one of the top all-time children's novels.

- Sergio Garcia burst onto the professional golf scene and dueled with Tiger Woods at the 1999 PGA Championship. However, he long carried the title, "best golfer to never win a Major championship". He had zero Major wins in 73 career starts. He even once claimed, *"I was not good enough to win a Major."* He shed that title by finally winning the Masters in 2017.

- Jack Canfield's best-selling book, *Chicken Soup for the Soul,* was rejected 144 times. He wrote, *"I encourage you to reject rejection. If someone says no, just say NEXT!"*

- In 1967, this musician got booed off the stage and was subsequently dropped from the tour where he was opening for The Monkees. His name was Jimi Hendrix.

- Hall of Fame coaches, Tom Landry, Bill Walsh, and Jimmy Johnson, collectively started off their NFL coaching careers with a record of 0-25.

- Steve Jobs was fired from the company that he founded only to be re-hired 11 years later. His return propelled Apple® to the elite status of innovation.

- Ellen Latham was fired at the age of 40 from her dream job as an exercise physiologist in 1996. Her comeback resulted in founding the franchise Orangetheory® fitness.

- Hillary Scott, *twice,* never made it past the preliminary stages on *American Idol*, meaning that she didn't even get to sing for the judges. She then founded Lady Antebellum and has since won 5 Grammy's.

- Mike Krzyzewski, during his first three seasons at Duke University, had an ACC record of just 13-29. He became the NCAA all-time winingest coach in basketball.

- Robert Downey Jr. had several years of headline-grabbing setbacks of drug-abuse and mistakes. He once was arrested for driving his Porsche naked with heroin, cocaine, and a loaded .357 magnum. His comeback has resulted in him now being looked upon as one of the best actors in history.

- Jan Koum and his mother moved to United States at the age of 16 from Kiev, Ukraine. They lived off government assistance and he swept floors at a local grocery store. He sold his company WhatsApp® at the age of 37 for approximately $7 billion.

It's not about the *setback*, it's about the *comeback*!

PROTECTION FROM LIGHTNING

"You don't throw an entire life away, just because they are banged up a little."—Tom Smith, Seabiscuit's trainer

LIGHTNING RODS DO not attract bolts of lightning. Lightning will strike regardless of the presence of a lightning rod.

A lightning rod serves to protect the structure from the strike.

It channels the lightning to the ground, saving the building from the brunt of the strike. [15]

Lightning strikes are so powerful that the structure needs a protector.

The lightning rod is the hinge that connects us with who we are going to become. The lightning rod in our lives is the person who protects us from the lightning strike. They either deflect the strike or encourage the person and build them back up.

Connection is the shared experience, relatedness, and the feeling of oneness with someone else. Connection with others is a primary need for us all. It is as important to our development as shelter and safety.

Connection is how we build our confidence.

The lightning rod serves as a connector between being told *"you're not good enough"* and someone telling you that *"you are good enough."*

If the lightning strike comes from a positive figure, the lightning rod will be someone close to us, someone willing to extend us grace and help us to see our true self. This might also be a coach, teacher, family member, inspirational figure, teammate, or colleague.

Just as everyone has had a setback in their life, everyone who has had a comeback also had *at least* one person who was able to support them and pick them back up. Just as the hinge moments mean we are only one opportunity away, we are also only one word of encouragement away from our comeback. The hinge people in our lives connect who we are currently with who we will become.

We all need people, and these examples are a just small sample of the lightning rod.

- Seabiscuit's original trainer, Sunny Jim, was an accomplished trainer with two Triple Crown winners. But he simply did not invest the time required to reveal the potential that this horse had. It was only when Seabiscuit's new owner and trainer, Tom Smith, took over that Seabiscuit became who he would become.

- After learning of yet another rejection for his first book, Dr. Seuss was on his way home to burn his manuscript when he ran into an old college buddy, Mike McClintock, on the street in New York City, who encouraged him to try again. Dr. Seuss stated, *"If I had been walking down the other side of Madison Avenue, I'd be in the dry-cleaning business today."*

- Robert Downey Jr. at his rock bottom was unemployable and uninsurable. It was Mel Gibson who took him in and provided him with a home and a lead role in a movie. Mel Gibson encouraged him to take responsibility and, if he embraced the part of his soul that was ugly, he would become a man of humility and his life would change.

Lightning rods save structures, but human lightning rods save lives.

Brooks Williams grew up in southwest Louisiana. She was a basketball player but she, like many young athletes, became injured in high school.

She hurt her knee while at Jennings High School and twice had arthroscopic surgery. A knee "scope" today is much less invasive and debilitating than in the 1980s and '90s. She missed almost two entire seasons in high school but, despite her injuries, she still earned all-state honors.

She followed a family tradition of attending Mississippi State University and walked onto the Mississippi State basketball team. Brooks' playing days were numbered due to her injuries, but coach Sharon Fanning saw and felt her passion. Brooks still ended up traveling with the team and becoming a glorified manager.

Brooks loved coaching and started with 9- and 10-year-olds. But, as she got older, she continued coaching older AAU teams during her time in college. She loved coaching and knew since she was young that she wanted to be a collegiate coach with her career.

She was young, impressionable, hungry, and eager.

What Brooks Williams couldn't have realized is that her hinge moment was about to come in the form of a lightning strike.

During the 1980s and '90s, the women's game of basketball centered around the two top women's programs, the University of Tennessee, led by iconic coach Pat Summit, and Louisiana Tech.

The Lady Techsters, as they were known, were a dynasty. They were the team that the University of Tennessee Lady Vols had to supplant to be the best. Louisiana Tech won 3 national championships and reached 13 final fours. They were the number #1 seed seven out of nine consecutive years in the NCAA tournament.

In of the state of Louisiana, women's basketball revolved around the Lady Techsters, and a huge part of the rise of the dynasty was because of Kim Mulkey.

Kim Mulkey was a southerner at heart and, as the daughter of a marine, she grew up hard-nosed. She played baseball with the boys as a youth and was simply the best on the team. She never missed even one day of school and graduated as valedictorian.

Kim Mulkey was a 5'4" point guard who knew about winning. The All-American made four straight final fours as a player at Louisiana Tech and ultimately finished with an amazing 130-6 record. She won a Gold Medal with the USA basketball team at the 1984 Olympic Games. When her playing days ended, she became the top assistant coach at Louisiana Tech.

She spent 15 seasons as an assistant and associate head coach at Louisiana Tech where she won a national championship and earned seven final four appearances.

Kim Mulkey would eventually win three national championships as the head coach of Baylor University. In doing so, she would become the *only* person to ever win national championships as a player, assistant coach, and a head coach.

Kim Mulkey's influence was legendary, especially in the state of Louisiana. She's impacted and transformed thousands of kids and lives through basketball. You could say she was more than a woman, but less than a goddess, kind of like Athena, the Greek goddess.

Her competitiveness and no-nonsense approach on the court was also legendary. She was a tough coach and with no filter, she spoke her mind.

Brooks Williams had just completed her freshman year in college and was still coaching her AAU team when she met coach Kim Mulkey. During one summer showcase tournament, she was helping out the collegiate coaches at an AAU event in Opelousas, Louisiana. She was taking care of the coaches, handing out rosters, food, and whatever they needed.

One of the coaches in the stands at this AAU tournament was Kim Mulkey. Brooks was like many kids, boys and girls alike, in the state of Louisiana—she idolized Kim.

So when Brooks was in the stands that day, confiding to the goddess of Louisiana basketball, Kim politely asked her what she wanted to do.

Brooks quickly and confidently replied, *"I want to do what you're doing, I want to coach in college."*

Kim blunt and directness came out in her reply. *"Well, you know Brooks, it's going to be tough for you to ever get in. You're not playing and this is a players' league."*

This was a positive lightning strike from "out of the blue."

Imagine hearing this directly from whoever your idol was. You probably would have had the same reaction as Brooks experienced. Now, Brooks was also a tough Louisiana kid with a similar competitive drive and mindset, but some things are tough to handle. Brooks admitted that she was crushed. She recalled that she was simply "heartbroken."

This coach, whom she had idolized for years and wanted to be her, had just told her that she *couldn't do it.*

How important was what transpired next? Brooks retreated behind the stands and behind closed doors, but she was followed by a lightning rod.

There was another coach who had heard the transaction. Pam Stackhouse was an assistant coach at Purdue University at the time. She would eventually win her own national championship in 1999 with the Boilermakers. "Stack" was also a tough Louisiana native and had coached with Kim Mulkey at Louisiana Tech.

Pam Stackhouse followed young Brooks around to the back of the arena after hearing the transaction. She told her the opposite. *"Look at my path, girl, you don't listen to that okay? You can be anything you want to be."*

Pam Stackhouse's journey into the coaching realm was also non-traditional, which is probably why she followed Brooks. She was not a collegiate player either and her path started as Director of Academic Services at Louisiana Tech. However, she worked the Lady Techsters summer basketball camps and so she got to know the entire coaching staff.

She ran the dormitories for the basketball players during the summer camps. One of the players whom she connected with and developed a bond with was Monica Maxwell, one of the top 5 players in the country.

Pam would turn in her phone bill to head basketball coach, Leon Barmore. He commented how Monica called her more often than any of the other coaches, and when another coaching position was available, he went directly to Pam and offered her the job. Her decision to accept the position on the staff was a hinge moment that made all of the difference in her non-traditional career path.

Three tough Louisiana women bonded together through a lightning strike. It came from Kim, hit Brooks directly, and Pam was the lightning rod.

Who knows why Kim spoke those honest words to Brooks that day in the bleachers. It was a bolt of positive lightning that struck hard out of the blue and made a profound impact. But it actually possessed truth inside of the message. It would indeed be tougher for Brooks than most to get into college coaching.

However, Brooks Williams either could listen to those words and believe them, or listen to them and believe in herself. And Brooks' dream became somewhat solidified that day. She decided to use that moment and become a Division I head coach.

Ironically, Kim Mulkey would eventually help Brooks land her very first collegiate coaching position. Coach Brooks Williams would indeed become a Division I head basketball coach. Kim, Pam, and Brooks kept the Louisiana bond together, remain friends, and continue to speak to each other regularly.

It's amazing sometimes how the connections in our life form.

When we have a setback, our connection with others is essential to the comeback.

During the difficult times that we faced, most likely there were others with us to guide us, walk with us, and support us. Or perhaps they just showed us enough grace that we could move forward without the shame or guilt. Our connection provided us with confidence and belief.

CONNECTION THROUGH OUR BROKENNESS

"The spiritual path is not a solo endeavor"—Tara Brach

IN THE 15TH century, the Japanese *shogun* was Yoshimasa.

The Shogunate was the military ruler of Japan, below only the emperor in terms of title. Yoshimasa enjoyed high culture and surrounded himself with artists and poets. He implemented the Japanese tea ceremony, which is still known today as the *way of tea*.

The way of tea is a symbolic "act of transformation." It is a spiritual practice ceremony, complete with dress, ritual, and arrangements. The ceremony itself represents peace, tranquility and harmony and much goes into the preparation.

Of highest importance are the actual tea bowls. The ceremonial host slowly fills the cups, and the presentation consists of the turning of the cups and handing them to the guests.

Once, a favorite tea bowl of Yoshimasa fell from his hands and broke. He immediately sent it to be repaired.

Yoshimasa chose the artisans in China, who were the experts of the day. The Chinese ceramists repaired it, but he was infuriated when it returned. It was mended, but his lovely tea bowl now had unsightly iron staples. [16]

The *shogun* then had the Japanese ceramists attempt to repair it. They mended the tea bowl, but the fractured lines were now highlighted with gold dust.

The artisans had created a masterful, more delightful way to fix broken items, and the art of Kintsukuroi was born. Kintsugi, shortened from *Kintsukuroi*, is translated as *"golden repair."*

Yoshimasa was so pleased because not only had the bowl been repaired, but also the imperfections were now emphasized, and the bowl itself became unique and reborn. Kintsugi allows the broken item to be revitalized into new life.

The custom is captivating because the fix isn't used to make it look like new again. Kintsugi actually becomes part of the history of the object because the repair is illuminated.

Most restorations are an attempt to cover up the imperfection, scratches, or breaks. However, Kintsugi became part of a worldview of the acceptance of imperfections.

Life is about the repair.
Life is about the comeback.

We are all broken. But do we hide our imperfections and lose the connection with others and isolate, or can we illuminate the repair?

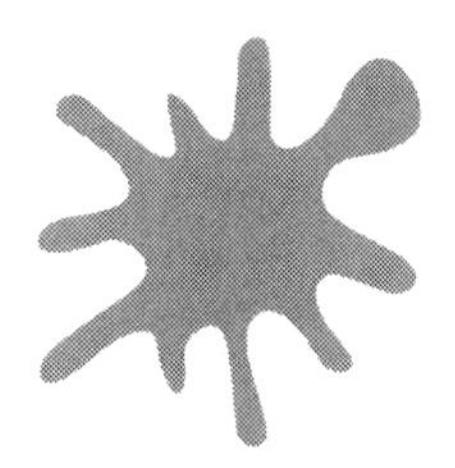

A MAN NAMED SAUL

"What hurts you, blesses you."—Rumi

THERE WAS A significant figure in history named Saul of Tarsus.

He was from a devout Jewish family and was considered "the best and the brightest." He was brought up in the best schools, had the best teachers, and was a man who was groomed to be a High Priest.

Saul was present and alive during the time of Jesus, even though they never met, and debated the authenticity of this man. Saul persecuted those who followed Jesus and his teachings. He was fanatical about entering homes of Christians and arresting them, even condemning them to death.

However, his goal to become High Priest took a drastic turn.

He was on his way to Damascus with others to again arrest and persecute Christians. As he drew near the city, a voice inquired: *"Saul, Saul, why do you continue to persecute me?"*

"Who are you, lord?" Saul asked. And the voice replied, *"I am Jesus, the one you are persecuting!"*[17]

Then Saul was struck blind by a literal *light from heaven* and instructed to go to Damascus to await further instructions.

Saul was led by hand into Damascus and he then went three days without food or water.

We can only imagine what these 72 hours were like for Saul. Struck blind and going without food or water, it must have been a dark time and one filled with reflection. Most likely, he was scared and confused, having a major *"what's next"* moment.

Chances are that we have all had the 72-hour experience of dread and despair. Those times of our life where we royally messed up, fell short, and questioned or became scared of what was next.

There are dark periods and valleys in all of our lives. We are faced with trying to pick up our own pieces, quiet the wake left behind us, and move forward. When we encounter these times, depression, anxiety, anger, hopelessness, and a myriad of other feelings step forward in our mind.

Nothing can prevent these valleys and we all experience them. Some of us respond differently and more severely to these tough situations.

Tragic events like death of a loved one, cancer, abuse, depression, bankruptcy, and catastrophic injuries can cause major emotional setbacks.

Through our connection with others is how we make a comeback.

A man named Ananias

Saul's life was solely focused on rising in status in the Jewish faith by persecuting Christians. He simply did not know what was coming next after he experienced Jesus on the road.

There was a man living in Damascus named Ananias. He received a vision from God as well, instructing him to go to Saul.

Saul was renowned for killing Ananias' own people. He was essentially a terrorist and was in Damascus to capture Christians and throw them in prison—and now Ananias was instructed to go to this man?

Ananias traveled to where Saul was staying and saw him blind and in despair. He put his hands on Saul saying, "*Brother Saul.*"[18]

Saul arose, and the scales fell off his eyes.

Ananias called Saul, the murderer and persecutor of Christians, *"Brother Saul"*. He connected Saul with who he was with who would eventually become. *"Brother Saul!"* Those words echo. And there is no ambiguity when calling someone "brother."

Ananias was the lightning rod for Saul.

Saul's conversion would led him to be known as Paul, the most famous Christian missionary the world has even seen.

Just as none of us can understand the impact that we make on someone else's life. Ananias could not fully grasp the impact that he would make on Paul's life or history.

We might not be called to use our gifts in the same manner that Paul did. But we can all be the person to connect someone with who they are supposed to become.

We all need an Ananias. Better still, we all can be an Ananias for others.

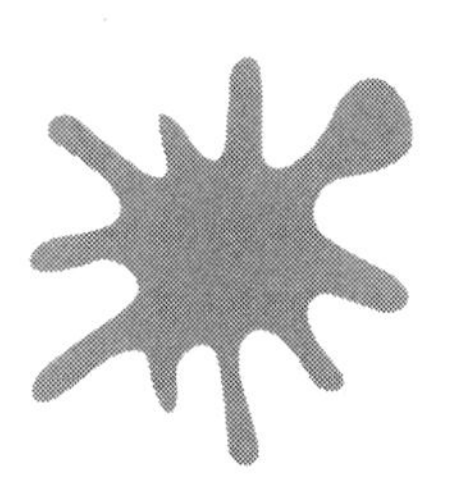

ILLUMINATING THE REPAIR

"There is a crack in everything, that's how the light gets in."—Leonard Cohen

RACHEL SUSSMAN'S ARTWORK is unique because she incorporates the practice of Kintsugi.

Those walking on the streets in New York City can literally see her artwork. It consists of mending the sidewalk cracks within specific parts of the city.

She loved the idea of something being more beautiful because it was broken. So she created sidewalk Kintsugi, in which she mended the streets with enamel and metallic dust, thus the streets actually became paved with gold.

As part of her art exhibit at the Des Moines Art Center, she mended an actual fissure in the museum's marble floor with gold.

Noticing the cracks.

Cracks are representations that something needs our attention, but we often don't notice them or want to notice them until they are in need of desperate repair!

Filmmaker, J. J. Abrams, in the *Star Wars* saga, *The Rise of Skywalker*, highlighted the internal struggle of the antagonist character, Kylo Ren. He emphasized the cracks in his repaired helmet. The cracks illustrated the imperfections both in the helmet and the struggle within himself.

Rachel's work illuminates the connection between periods of time. She remarks that over time *"even the repairs will be destroyed."* Such is the transient nature of everything, over time. [19]

During the summer, the full bloom of a tree is gorgeous, the shade it provides is rewarding, and it glorifies the overall health of the earth. Then the season changes into autumn and with it, the leaves morph color. Before winter comes and the leaves fall, the trees produce an even more breathtaking scene.

Even though the leaves are dying, senior pictures are taken to illuminate the season of life. We relish in the beauty of the leaves' life cycle and basic imperfection.

Our lives are the same way, filled with imperfection.

And while our experiences do not define us, they do influence us.

There will be many breaks and cracks in our own façade. These blemishes are often more emotional, spiritual, and social than they are aesthetic. They delve way deeper than just projecting our own cosmetic image to others.

How many people are at parties discussing how empty they feel inside, how loneliness creeps in, or that their relationships are horrible?

That would be awkward.

Rather, we spend time trying to manage our image instead of accentuating our flaws. However, in our own close circles of relationships, we hide those same issues instead of sharing them.

We cover up instead of confide in.

We isolate instead of connect with.

The strength and nourishment of friends and those who we can confide in and connect with is how we repair ourselves.

The art of Kintsugi, the golden repair, occurs through the connection with others. Reaching out to others and assisting them by sharing our own story of struggle and redemption is how we help our own brokenness.

We can't help anyone else in life without also helping ourselves.

Share your story

Sandy Zimmerman grew up in Tacoma, Washington and did not have it easy growing up. She grew up poor and, with her family on welfare assistance, she even spent time in the foster care system. She also experienced many forms of abuse as a child.

She vaulted herself into sports at a young age as an escape, and Judo became her focus. She started training at the age of five. Judo is a sport of grit and where you will get tapped out; it's just a matter of how often. The fortitude lies in answering the question–can you keep coming back?

She received coaching, trained hard, and propelled herself to the national level. At the age of 12, she won the Judo USA national championship

She was both sad and happy after winning the title.

She was sad because the girls who finished second and third were taking pictures with their family and friends, and she was alone. But she was also happy because she at least had her sensei with her that day.

Her sensei told her immediately they came off the podium, *"Sandy, you can go to the Olympics."* It was timely because just then Women's Judo was being introduced to the Olympics.

Her thoughts at the time were, *"Girls like me don't dream those dreams, my goal for today is that maybe I can go to bed tonight and not be hungry or get beaten."*

When you are abused as a child, it negatively impacts your confidence. It's tough to simply have the mental capacity to make sense of and handle it. We inherently ask ourselves, "*Was it my fault?*" And, "*How are people going to judge me?*"

Sadly, that dream of the Olympics and the sensei who served as a lightning rod came to an immediate halt just two weeks after her win at the national championship.

Her father sat her and her two brothers down in the driveway and told them that they were leaving town and Mom was not going with them. So each of the three kids got a corner of the trailer for their few things and off they went. They had no money, only stopping for bread and bologna, and moved across the entire state of Washington. The closest dojo was now two hours away.

Judo was finished.

Sandy now lived in a trailer in small town of about 500 people. She immersed herself into the sport of basketball. She played all the time and a coach found her and poured into her the same way the sensei had done. Receiving a basketball scholarship at a Division I school with a high-school graduating class of just sixteen kids is a pretty big dream.

It doesn't matter where you come from, what you've gone through, or what you're going through. You can still dream big dreams.

Even when she injured her knee during her junior season in the tiny high school, she still earned a basketball scholarship at Gonzaga University. "Dream Big Dreams" would still echo.

For years and years, she would hear the little voice in her head tell her, *"Share your story! Share your story!"* Early on, however, she would snap back quickly to that voice shouting, *"Hell no! It's embarrassing!"*

Sandy became a physical education teacher, married, and had a family of her own with three children. But, she still fought the shame for years.

She didn't even share her secrets with her husband of many years. But as she grew up, even though the negative voice persisted, the positive voice grew louder. After she continued to dissent to the negative voice, the positive voice would conclude with *"Yeah, but it has a happy ending."*

Instead of carrying around a shameful secret for her entire life, she began to wear it as a badge of honor! She illuminated the repair and began to share it.

What happened that she was now able to share it?

It was after watching a single episode of the TV show *American Ninja Warrior* that another dream was planted. Almost immediately, they got to work and built obstacles in their back yard to practice and simulate the course.

Sandy earned an opportunity to try out and stepped up to the start line during season 11 of the awesome show.

It was not her first attempt, however.

During seasons eight and nine of the show, she attempted the course, but did not make it past the second obstacle. She was injured, had surgery, and could not even compete during season 10.

Could she now overcome and navigate those two voices that battled it out for her own headspace? One voice was still the scared, timid, little girl who grew up on welfare and spent time in foster care. The other voice, however, was a strong, confident, 42-year-old woman and mother of three.

What was different now during season 11 of *American Ninja Warrior* was that even though the two voices in her head still battled it out, she was able to now *tell* herself what she was going to do.

Her goal was not to think about the end and the mountaintop, but instead to focus on the process, which was take it one obstacle at a time, and just breathe.

By focusing on her process, Sandy Zimmerman became the first mother to ever hit the buzzer on *American Ninja Warrior* and complete the course.

It was the successful journey that provided Sandy the strength to finally share her story that already had a happy ending.

Illuminate the repair.

It's not about the *setback*, it's about the *comeback*!

Illuminating the repair means building our confidence through connection with others despite our brokenness.

Hayden Hurst was a teenage, multi-sport, all-star athlete. The six foot five inch 245 lb right-handed baseball pitcher signed a $400,000 signing bonus with the Pittsburgh Pirates after being drafted. However, his first professional start at the age of 19 also became his last.

He spent three struggling years with the team.

As sometimes happens, he could no longer locate his pitches in the strike zone. One day he even accidently hit a batter in the head with a 94 mph fastball. He developed anxiety on the field and depression off it.

He did what we all do when faced with a loss of identity and confidence, he isolated. He spent his days off the field in a dark room watching television. Not even the closest people to him knew the extent of what he was dealing with.

> *"It's such a darkness that comes over you," Hurst says of the depression. "You don't want to go anywhere or do anything... and I don't wish it upon anybody."* [20]

At the lowest point, his minor league pitching coach, Scott Elarton, called Hayden's parents and told them they needed to go see their son.

At the beginning of his third year of professional baseball, he simply left the game. He was twenty-two years old. On his way out of the Pirates organization, the director of minor league baseball operations, Larry Broadway, shared a bolt of lightning with him: *"I hope there's something you can stick to in your life."* [20]

Hayden spent time researching what had transpired with his own mental wellness. He also decided that he would now play football and he walked onto the football team at the University of South Carolina.

He was an explosive athlete whose backbone was as strong as his wishbone. He simply competed and worked and did everything the right way. Where baseball was slow moving for him, football was explosive, and he relished it. He became a tight end on the team and in two seasons only dropped two passes, while also earning first team All-SEC honors.

He became one of the country's top tight ends and was drafted in the first round by the Baltimore Ravens.

His story is remarkable for his ability to share his brokenness to help other people.

He developed the Hayden Hurst Family Foundation, which is designed to assist kids with mental health awareness. This platform is used to create a dialogue around mental health issues and mental illness.

The biggest contributor to connection is through talking with people, getting it out there, and addressing the issue.

Illuminate the repair.

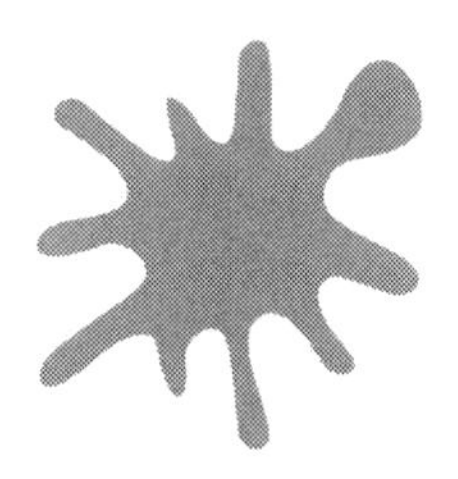

PROCESS > PRODUCT

> *"I see the mountains in the distance that I long to climb, but first I must pack up my fear and leave it behind."*—Jennae CeCelia

PEOPLE HAVE DEBATED for centuries the journey versus the destination.

First, we wouldn't embark on a worthwhile journey without a destination. The destination is what makes us dig deep and persevere in the face of extreme adversity.

We play to win the game!

However, the path itself and the effort necessary to reach the destination is the essence of life. The journey is what contains the meaning in life.

We can't have the glory without the guts. Being able to suffer and endure demands so much that we have to ask ourselves, would it be worth all of the turmoil even if we did not reach the destination?

Gil Reyes, Andre Agassi's lifetime strength coach, shares an epic quote: *"Some battles aren't worth fighting even if you win, but most battles are worth fighting even if you lose."*

It means that if you had a vision, would it be worth pursuing even if you failed? That of course is not the mindset heading into the journey, but that is just the question that needs to be continually answered *(more than once)* on the journey.

Would the struggle be worth it even if you lost?

Mountains are significant in almost every culture.

The top of Mount Olympus in Greece, for instance, was the home of the Greek Gods and Greek mythology. Mount Sinai in Egypt was the place where Moses received the Ten Commandments. In the Hindu and Buddhist cultures, Mount Kailash serves as the sacred mountain in Tibet. This mountain is forbidden from being climbed, it serves as a pilgrimage for those around the base.

There are scores of sacred mountains on earth. Mountains provide an intersection between cultures, landscapes, and the history of a region.

People climb the mountain to experience the divinity, but they come back down to experience humanity.

The most symbolic part of almost any mountain is the peak. If you look at a mountain from a distance, it looks small. Even as you drive into and view a city's landscape, it looks small. But the closer you get to it, the larger and larger it becomes.

When we are at the base of a mountain, it looks its biggest, and it is natural to gaze at the top peak *(if you can)* and perhaps even think it's un-climbable.

But once the journey up the mountain begins, as a climb or hike, an interesting shift takes place; we no longer become fixated on the top itself. We now look at the next step in our climb and where we need to place our foot.

Sure, we may take a peek at the summit, but mostly we look at the ground at our feet. And we also start to look at how far we have come.

Our focus adjusts once again.

Our feelings change as we look at the base of the mountain that we've climbed. Perhaps during our climb, looking at the ground causes us to reflect and appreciate our climb even more.

Who knows, maybe we think too far ahead and wonder about getting down before we have even climbed up. But, perhaps hopefully, looking at how far we've come inspires us and provides a renewed drive to keep moving forward.

And during this entire journey, while our viewpoint and feelings have adjusted, the mountain has not changed, even a little bit. The mountain hasn't changed, only how we look at it.

On our own journey that we are on, the goal may seem huge at the base. We may not even know how we are going to achieve it. But once we start to move towards our goal, our viewpoint changes.

The issue isn't that we focus on the outcome. The trouble arises when we *only* focus on the outcome. In our own lives, we *only* focus on the results, how things are going to work out, and whether we will *make* it.

But our obsession with the product takes us away from the process, our immediate reality, and situation.

Think of the cause of your greatest stressor in life right now. There is an outcome that we haven't reached. Perhaps we want to lose 10 lbs, earn a certain income or statistic, rid ourselves of a bad habit, or even meet someone special.

We want the results!
We want the win!
We want it to work out exactly how we want it to!

We want the spoils and accolades from our hard work and toil. We all want the positives.

However, a focus only on winning doesn't lead to winning, a focus on the process does. Results are like the sun, we can glance at it, but we can't stare at it.

Our ability to focus is how we build our confidence. But, our ability to refocus uncovers our level of confidence. Can you focus on the process or does the product completely cloud your view?

FALSE SUMMITS

"Our viewpoint changes depending upon where we stand."—C. S. Lewis

ANOTHER INTERESTING OCCURRENCE takes place that alters our experience. Depending on the size of the goal, we may think we've reached the peak, when in reality we haven't.

Climbers think they have reached the top of the mountain, but it isn't the true summit. These false peaks are dangerous because of the predicament that the climbers can find themselves in.

These are false summits.

False peaks are usually very comfortable spots and the climber thought it was the top right up until the moment that they arrived.

Some people at these false summits have decided to stop.

They've been climbing for hours, are tired, and had their eyes looking at the summit, only to have their hopes come smack back into the reality that they need to go higher. If there is no veteran with them and the climbing is tough (which it almost always is), then it becomes too easy to simply stop right there.

There are many false summits in life. We will often have false summits on the way to the mountaintop.

The fake peaks occur when we've reached a goal, set a personal best or record, or went further than we have before. The extreme difficulty in overcoming false peaks exists because our mind once again simply wants us to be safe and stop. Our own defenses to fight are weakest when we are tired and have reached some sort of peak or goal. It's natural to relax and enjoy it.

But the effect and satisfaction of reaching peaks eventually wears off.

It's not about the peak itself, but rather the climb.

THE MOUNTAIN TOP EXPERIENCE

"I don't wanna come back down from this cloud."—Gavin Rossdale

THE TREE LINE in Colorado is at around 12,000 feet. It simply gets too cold, too much snowfall and ice, too windy, and too short of a growing season for trees to grow. However, people love hiking above the tree line and reaching the mountaintop because of the feeling of accomplishment, peace, serenity, and view.

Close above the actual line in Colorado lives the oldest known species of tree, the Bristlecone Pine. This tree defines the tree line.

Some of these pine trees are over 5,000 years old, which means they were around when Julius Caesar was alive!

This tree is indeed tough because it survives in the worst type of environment. However, the Bristlecone pine tree is small. Due to its environment on the mountaintop, it takes *centuries* to gain full maturity.

It represents where real growth takes place.

Such is life.

The real growth occurs in the valley, not on the mountaintops.

We can't spell "growth" without "ow."

The tough times, the struggle, the setbacks, and the journey is where real growth and appreciation happens. We can only truly appreciate and have gratitude for that which is acquired through hard work and toil. The harder we work for something, the more we will enjoy it.

It is not ideal going through the hardships, just as hanging out in the valley the entire hike isn't much fun either. The mountaintop experience is great, but it is temporary.

We will spend more time hiking the actual mountain than taking pictures at the top.

Mount Everest for many is the Super Bowl of climbers. It takes an average of 40 to 60 days of climbing to reach the peak. Climbers must acclimate themselves to reach the highest peak in the world, and the weather must be ideal for a successful summit. There is only a small window of time every year when the summit can be achieved.

To illustrate the mountaintop fallacy, people spend forty days of actual climbing to the top of Mount Everest at 29,029 feet. Not to mention all of the resources and preparation during the months prior to the attempt to reach the peak. But the amount of time a climber spends at the top is only 10-15 minutes.[22]

It is an incredible view from the top, and it took a mighty amount of preparation and resources to accomplish such a feat. But mountaintop experiences do not last, and we have to come back down.

You can't spend much time at all enjoying the view.

We can't live on the mountaintop. The climb and ascent is more important than the peak.

Tragically, most deaths occur on the descent of Everest. Research reveals that seventy-three percent of deaths take place on the way down the mountain. That's when severe fatigue or the belief that "*I've done it*" sets in.

What have been your own mountaintop experiences in life, and how long did they really last? Was it a graduation, vacation, a successful race, or even a wedding?

Was there a letdown or comedown from the mountaintop?

Did the wedding bells slowly turn into the wedding blues?

It's natural. There are so many months of wedding preparation, anticipation, and communication into a life-changing event that after it is over, there's sadness.

We get so consumed, that the wedding day bliss sometimes becomes more important than the marriage.

Olympians experience the mountaintop fallacy as well. The vision, the disciplined weekly training schedules, the training groups, sacrifices, overcoming the mental challenges, and simply preparing for the games, leads many to experience depression when it's over, even if they received a medal.

It leads people to the feeling after the mountain top of "*okay, now what?*"

What keeps us striving and enjoying the process is through our relationships and connection with others.

WHY THE PROCESS IS MORE IMPORTANT

IRVIN AND BONITA had four children. However, growing up in rural Mississippi, no one was close in proximity to their 52-acre property so their kids were always playing with one another. The four brothers of this family would become better athletes than most in the area, and there were quite a few trips to the ER over the years.

Irv was the patriarch of the family and was a hard-nosed, old school football coach. He coached for 28 years and his toughness rubbed off on his own boys, who were all quarterbacks at the high school.

One of middle sons would become the best athlete of the bunch, but he only received one scholarship offer to play quarterback at the University of Southern Mississippi. And that was only after another player de-committed.

This quarterback was passionate and competitive, and once he was put into a collegiate game he never looked back. Brett Favre entered a game in which they trailed, and led the team to a 31-24 comeback victory.

Favre's intensity and toughness would be the cornerstone for all of his playing days.

He had a near-fatal car accident the summer before his senior season at Southern Mississippi and he had part of his intestines removed. Yet he only missed one game. His first game back and nowhere near healthy, he led his team to an upset victory over vaulted Alabama.

The Atlanta Falcons picked Brett Favre in the second round of the 1991 NFL draft. Unfortunately, Brett Favre's first professional completed pass was intercepted and ran for a touchdown. He was traded after just one season to the Green Bay Packers.

Favre was confident. But his leadership and toughness was legendary because he made others around him better.

The 1992 season did not start off well, but he started the third game of the season after the starter Don Majkowski was injured. He stated before the season began, *"Once I'm in it's going to be over. I really believe it."* [23] After his first start with the Green Bay Packers, Brett Favre would remain the starting quarterback for an NFL record of 253 consecutive games.

He led the Packers to back-to-back playoff appearances, something that had not been accomplished since the late 1960s. During the 1995 season, he would become the NFL's MVP and lead the Packers to one win away from the Super Bowl.

Favre separated his shoulder during a game that MVP season and the injury began his use of painkillers. He quickly developed a dependency and was taking fourteen pills a day before receiving help. In May 1996, months after winning the MVP and propelling his team to the brink of greatness, he checked into a treatment facility.

Favre would once again come back from this setback. The 1996 season was his best yet, winning his second consecutive MVP and leading the Packers to their first Super Bowl Championship since 1967.

Favre revitalized the entire Green Bay franchise. They had no playoff appearances in many years before he arrived, and he took them to ten. He won three straight NFL MVP trophies, had eleven pro-bowl appearances, and broke numerous records.

Brett Favre squeezed every drop out of his potential through his ability to come back.

He started 321 straight games, including the playoffs. That was 18½ seasons without missing a start. The numerous injuries that he had and played through included a broken foot, broken hand, separated shoulder, sprained knees, torn biceps, and concussions, to mention a few.

Favre's determination and confidence drove him to success, but the fuel was his passion towards the game. He approached it with a child-like love, and that was his most endearing quality. A child approaches the game not with weighty expectations in mind, but simply to have fun and meet the challenge at hand.

So, how does Brett Favre's story demonstrate why the process is more important than the product?

The ultimate achievement of a professional football player and team has to be winning the Super Bowl and holding up the Lombardi trophy. That is the goal of every organization.

The Super Bowl is the pot of gold at the end of the rainbow.

But Brett Favre proved that more important than the gold was the rainbow itself.

Any award, recognition, or accomplishment was not as important as the actual process of getting there. His career represented proof that the process is more important than the actual product.

Stating that the process is more important than the product does not mean that the gold at the end of the rainbow is unimportant.

The pot of gold would be nice, too.

We still play to win the game. No one would say that losing the Super Bowl is better than winning. Just because the process is more important takes nothing away from the product itself. Since the mountaintop becomes our focus and goal, it shows how utterly crucial the process actually is.

Brett Favre's passion resulted in him being a very emotional player. He once remarked how he cried after wins and cried after losses. But after he won the Super Bowl in 1996, he had a different reaction.

> *"Here I am in the greatest win of my career, standing on the podium thinking, 'This is it?' I shouldn't be feeling this."* [24]

Brett Favre commented how, during Coach Holmgren's locker room speech to the celebrating team, he just slipped off into the shower.

Why would he feel this negative emotion after supposedly the best and most important win of his career?

Excuse me, Mr. Favre, what do you mean, *"Is that it?!"*

Favre's response was strikingly eerily similar to many others who have reached the pinnacle of their career.

Bill Walsh, one of the greatest football coaches of all time, had a similar reaction to Favre. Immediately after winning his third Super Bowl with the San Francisco 49ers, the team of the '80s, he knew he was finished with coaching.

Coach Walsh was in the locker room during the winning Super Bowl celebration and Brent Musburger approached him for an interview. The locker room party was going on all around them and he posed the question, *"Was this your last game coaching?"*

Bill Walsh didn't answer the question and instead started crying and hugged his son because he knew it was over. Bill Walsh said later, *"I immediately felt like an outsider, no longer part of the team."* This feeling was just moments after his third championship.

Chuck Noll won four Super Bowls as coach of the Pittsburgh Steelers. He changed the entire city and revitalized the civic pride in the steel city. It was the team of the entire decade of the '70s. Yet he remarked how he would experience depression for about a month after the ultimate victories.

The Cowboys won three Super Bowls in four years in the 1990s. After the third championship, safety, Darren Woodson, stated it was relief, *"Thank God the season is over."*

When the Denver Broncos won their back-to-back Super Bowls in the 1997 and 1998 seasons, offensive guard, Mark Schlereth, commented on the win, *"It was a relief."*

Perhaps looking at the reactions of some of the ultimate mountain top experiences reveals some sort of truth. Why would these winners, Super Bowl champions, feel this emotional turmoil after the best moment of their career?

Again, why would Brett Favre ask himself rhetorically, "*Is this it?*"

It is the mountain top fallacy.

It is the basic belief that when I reach the ultimate goal (the top), my life will be complete. Or, I'll feel *this* certain way.

Winning and ultimate success and achievement is the mountaintop experience!

We overestimate the feeling of accomplishment and we underestimate the pain of anguish.

We can't Google an experience. We think we know what it will feel like when we reach the mountaintop, but in reality, we can't know. And even if we have an idea of what it may feel like, success only feeds a certain part of who we are.

The mountaintop experience feeds our ego, but not always our soul.

Brett Favre's passion, confidence, and toughness had propelled him to success. When it actually occurred, it meant that it was *over.* Even though they had won the championship, he didn't want it to end.

He stated, "*What you remember most is not so much the game, it's the journey. You remember the games that got you there, the practices, the bus rides.*"[24]

The rainbow itself was more important than the gold at the end of it.

After the championship, he immediately thought of the entire season and the comeback victory after losing back-to-back games. He relished the wins, but also the practical joke that they played on Coach during Halloween. He simply didn't want to come back down.

What professional or high-level athletes and coaches miss after their career has ended is always the same. What they miss most is the locker room camaraderie, the bus rides, and hanging out with their teammates.

They reflect on their connection with others. They appreciate the relationships.

You may or may not reach the top, that's the challenge, and success is not guaranteed. However, what sustains and lasts way beyond when performing is over are the connections. To suffer with one another, to celebrate, and to enjoy each other is why the process is most important.

When speaking to all of the NFL strength coaches at the Scouting Combine, I asked them to think about the Super Bowl championship that they each had won. I asked them to close their eyes and visualize an image of what came to mind.

I jokingly asked if they saw themselves alone holding the trophy in a large tub with bubbles all around them. Or did they view the adversity that was overcome and the relationships on the team?

Every single one of Super Bowl winning coaches had the same response, they thought about the relationships, overcoming the setbacks, and the connectivity with one another.

Even coaches who did not win the ultimate prize but had many years of success in the National Football League, mentioned the same theme.

The process is more important than the product because of the relationships that you develop on the journey.

REGRETS OF A DYING LIFE

"Everyone misses their friends when dying."—Bronnie Ware

BRONNIE WARE SPENT many years unfulfilled and occupied a variety of jobs. She experienced extreme loneliness and pain, and it became unbearable at times for her.

Bronnie didn't want to live because of the constant ache in her heart, and began writing her "exit" letter. The following evening, she received a call *out of the blue* from an old friend. They spoke for hours and her strength began to return.

We make connection through our brokenness.

She was now on a mission to find meaningful work. She simply wanted to live out her full worth.

Even with no formal qualifications, she became a palliative care nurse. As a nurse, she would have multiple intimate conversations with people during their last few weeks of life, and as a result her own life would be converted.

Bonnie was the one who was blessed to hear the anguish and pain that her patients had experienced. *It's in giving that we actually receive.*

Bronnie Ware wrote an international best seller, entitled *The Top 5 Regrets of The Dying: A Life Transformed By The Dearly Departing.* It has been read by over a million people and translated into 32 different languages. These honest conversations about life and death led to reflections about what these patients would have done differently.

Regret is a fascinating and powerful emotion. As she writes, *"It provides nothing but suffering because we are allowing the past to dictate our present."*[25]

We all have regret in life, and the negative emotion can be revealed in as young as two-year-olds. So we are all familiar with the feeling of the emotion. It's painful, we ask "what-if" questions, and we seek out what we would have done differently or why this event or person happened. Regret can cause us to doubt ourselves, our ability, and to avoid taking chances. It is a setback.

One of the top regrets from those in palliative care was, *"I wish I had stayed in touch with my friends."*

This is a significant regret because it has to do with others. It was revealed to these dying individuals that, in the end, the only things that mattered were love and our relationships.

Acquaintances seem to be commonplace in life. Even warm acquaintances in life play a role. They are in our life for a certain purpose and time.

Friendships remain precious because friends accept us as we are, not as others want us to be. Friendships that last the test of time and endure are invaluable.

Friends are there during the most difficult of times and through our pain. They are also there for the celebrations. They help us rally!

Bronnie uncovered that almost every regret came down to a lack of courage. In order to create a life with no regret one needs to have courage and faith. We have to be willing to take the risk. We can use regret as a beneficial positive emotion and a reference point moving forward. In order to make a comeback, we must have compassion toward ourselves and give ourselves permission to enjoy our own lives.

Faith isn't really faith until it's all we've got.

A SAILBOAT IS OFF COURSE 99% OF THE TIME

"I think failure is nothing more than life nudging you that you are off course."—Sara Blakey

IN THE OPEN ocean, sailboats are in a constant state of flux.

The weather, wind speed and direction, water currents and crosscurrents, all cause changes in the course. The faster the boat is moving, the more precise each movement becomes by the captain.

It is easy to get off course. Over many nautical miles, a variation of less than one degree at the start can cause the final destination to be miles away at the end.

Sailboats were made to come back.

A sailboat finds its destination by making course corrections along the way. Only by adjusting to the wind can they reach their final destination.

Tacking is how they do it, a series of zigzagging maneuvers that captains perform to use the wind and stay on course.

As humans, it is very easy to get off course. We are much like a sailboat because we were also designed to come back. It's how we find our destination.

This twenty-eight year old female swimmer had an extreme vision. She was a marathon swimmer, which meant hours upon hours of swimming in open water. She first accomplished fame by swimming around Manhattan, a total of twenty-eight miles.

Diana Nyad's bold vision was to be the first person to swim the 110 miles from Cuba to the Florida Keys. The challenge possessed many elements outside of just the actual swimming, including navigation, weather conditions, current flow, sharks, and the potential deadly jellyfish. The greatest ultra-swimmers had been attempting this feat since 1950, but it still had not been achieved.

Her first unsuccessful attempt was in 1978 as a twenty-eight year old. Unfortunately, after seventy-eight miles of swimming, the team had to pull her out because they were too far off course. Instead, she decided to turn her efforts towards the east of the Gulf of Mexico, and swam 102 miles from the Bahamas to the Florida coast. She completed the swim and decided it would be her last competitive marathon swim.

Her dream lay dormant for over 30 years!

However, when a dream awakens you from normal life, you have to pursue it, or battle with the regret.

In 2010, at the age of 60, the dream was rekindled. Diana Nyad began training again for the near impossible Cuba to United States swim. It took undaunted physical dedication and courage. She began her six- to seven-hour-long training swims and progressed to 14- and 15-hour ocean swims.

Her audacious goal was still to be the first person to ever complete the epic swim from Cuba to the United States without a shark cage.

The distress she would face during her journey included hypothermia, hallucinations, dehydration, shoulder pain, and mental fatigue, and yes, vomiting.

The amount of seawater that one swallows during marathon swims causes the body to simply retch.

Puke
&
Rally.

Nothing great is easy.

Her second attempt in 2011 also failed. She was pushed so far off course by the wind that after swimming for 40 straight hours, the distance to finish was still too great.

During her next attempt, she encountered the deadly boxed jellyfish that stung her with the most dangerous venom in the entire ocean. She was stung so badly that she suffered partial paralysis and was in danger of suffocating. It was a life-threating situation and she was pulled from the ocean to prevent drowning.

In 2012, thunderstorms caused 8-foot swells. After fifty-one hours of swimming, she had only covered 55 miles. The weather once again had pushed her so far off course that she had to be pulled out.

Her fourth attempt brought another disappointment, and in addition it fractured the team. The team had spent almost as many hours preparing as Diana had swimming and training. They were a volunteer army and all had lives outside of this amazing adventure. Trying to get every detail dialed in, like the nuances of feeding, water currents, and preventing deadly jellyfish stings, took its toll on many of the team members.

Everyone on the team experienced heartache and hardship.

In 2013, before her fifth attempt, almost everyone, even some of those in her own team, had said, "*It can't be done.*"[26]

However, on September 2, 2013, after 52 hours and fifty-four minutes of continuous swimming, fighting off boxed jellyfish, throwing up from the saltwater, and even hallucinating about seeing the Taj Mahal during the endeavor, she made it.

At 64 years old, Diana Nyad swam 110 miles from Havana, Cuba to Key West, Florida. Her journey started in 1978, but it was not completed until 2013.

One of the most awe-inspiring feats of all time took 36 years to complete, and she was able to do it because she wasn't about the setback, she was about the comeback.

It was only "nearly" impossible.

Fewer of us would have heard of Diana Nyad had she quit after her fourth attempt. But, have you ever heard the awesome story about the person who quit? Neither has anyone else!

It's the one mistake that crushes our own goals. It's the one mistake that can cause us to quit. If we can overcome the one crucial mistake, then we can come back.

When you dream big dreams and have audacious goals—a tall mountain to climb, a long race to run, or achievement to master—you'll have focus only for the short term and your process. During your climb, there will be steep cliffs, strong winds, and false summits.

Your journey will be tough.

It will be harder than you think and you will have setbacks. No matter what, you will have adversity, obstacles, and you'll want to quit. You are going to have to continue tacking, making adjustments, connecting with others, having courage, and never, ever giving up.

You don't have to know exactly how you'll reach your destination, just a relentless attitude and commitment to keep moving forward.

The good news is that it only takes one for a comeback. It only takes one person, one moment, or one decision to make all the difference.

OUR IDENTITY

"The value of our identity is that so often, it comes with purpose."—Richard Grant

IN 1973, SECRETARIAT won the Kentucky Derby and the Preakness Stakes, and was just one race away from winning the Triple Crown. Before the Belmont Stakes, Secretariat had become a national celebrity and was donned on the cover of *Times* magazine. It was a relief for citizens to follow him because, at the time, news about the Vietnam War and Watergate was bombarding everyone.

On June 9th, 1973, Secretariat went off as the favorite at 1-10 odds, which meant a $2 bet would win only about $0.20. The race in New York State took place in front of a crowd of almost 70,000 people and was watched on television by over 15 million households.

Secretariat did not disappoint and his performance became known as the greatest ever by a racehorse. He won the race by an astonishing margin of 31 lengths! He also set the record at 2:24 flat for the 1½-mile race, which still stands today. Many who had placed bets on Secretariat simply did not cash them in and instead kept them as souvenirs.

Secretariat only ran a few other races after the Belmont Stakes and won most of them, but his career was cut short and he did not race as a four-year-old.

The last race that Secretariat ran was the Canadian International Stakes in Toronto. His owner, Penny Chenery, paid homage to her trainer, Lucien Laurin, and jockey, Ron Turcotte, who were both Canadian. Secretariat won the race, and afterwards he was taken to another racetrack and paraded around the track to a crowd of 32,000 cheering fans. [27]

Secretariat merely ran a tribute lap, but what happened next added to the folklore of Secretariat.

Once the run was over, Secretariat instinctively walked over to stand in the winner's circle!

Secretariat's identity was one of a winner.

Is your identity of someone who can Puke & Rally?

Do you believe that it's about the comeback or have the setbacks kept you back?

It is tempting to discount the examples in this book, the stories of those who suffered and their comebacks. But they each developed and grew an identity of people who would overcome and comeback. They possessed belief.

How do we go from a pessimistic, negative, or angry mindset to a future self that we really want but are afraid to achieve?

The bridge is honesty.

You'll need to be truthful with yourself and believe that your identity is one of a winner. There is a saying that the truth hurts. It hurts because the truth is that we can always get better.

Rigorous honesty is painful. It is difficult to examine our past mistakes and still be able to create a vision for ourselves that knows it is one of a winner.

How can we believe that we are a winner when others have told us that we are not, or our past mistakes or circumstances show us that we are average?

Since it is difficult to believe, we cover it up instead and tell ourselves lies about our own identity because it protects our mind. When our mind discredits our true identity, it causes us not to try as hard, to dismiss others' success, or to operate without confidence. And we continue to tell ourselves lies.

The pies of lies that we tell ourselves are numerous, hidden, and very powerful. A small slice of these lies include:

> *"I didn't really care if I lost the weight."*
>
> Or
>
> *"If I only had 'this', then I would be happy."*
>
> Or
>
> *"If people knew my real issues, then they wouldn't like me."*
>
> Or
>
> *"I am only as good as my performance."*
>
> Or
>
> *"My life is this way because…"*

Or

"Those people are special examples, I'm not like that."

We all listen to these lies, so it's not a matter of *if* we tell ourselves lies. It's how frequent, severe, and deep rooted these beliefs are about ourselves.

It becomes impossible to face reality with confidence when our identity is skewed and, as a result, we'll never have the courage to change.

Now, the lies that we tell ourselves do have some truth in them. Yes, you have messed up. Yes, your circumstance was unfair. Yes, it will be very hard. Yes, your goals will be extremely difficult.

You will puke.

But, no matter how painful our experiences, these lies do not tell the whole truth.

However, you'll need to accept short-term discomfort for long-term gain.

In order to do this, we have to know our identity.

If we only identify with our performance, then we have to keep performing well to feel good about ourselves. Even the best results are temporary, and how we feel about ourselves can't have anything to do with what other people think of us.

If we only listen to what others say about us then we are slaves to other people's opinions of us. When we care too much about what others think, we will be left feeling empty.

If our identity is not rooted in something larger than our performance, we will continue to chase the result and only be able to use the result to feel good about ourselves. But it won't last for very long.

Hall of Fame golfer, Bernhard Langer, won his first major championship at the Masters. He stated, *"It was a wonderful feeling, but there was still a void there. It was almost a feeling of emptiness."*

Langer wondered, *"Is this all there is? I had lots of money, fast cars, a couple of homes, and a young wife. Basically, all you could dream of in this world."*[28]

It was his first Major championship, and he didn't know why he felt empty.

A performance-driven life is a vicious cycle and we all have it to a degree. It's a huge driving factor, to be as good as we possibly can be and to be recognized for it. However, performance is based on the belief that I am only as good as my results.

If your own identity is rooted in wins and losses and only on your performance, then no matter how lofty the goal or high the mountain peak, the feeling of emptiness will only depart temporarily. Even when we do perform well, that effect lasts only so long. Soon, anxiety and stress enter back into the fray.

And when we are not successful, the void magnifies after losses and setbacks.

There will be mishaps, setbacks, and pain. If we only connect with the failures, then we will think the setback is our real identity, which is not true.

Our identity must be rooted in something larger than our performance.

For Bernhard Langer, only after he developed a relationship with his higher power of Christ did he understand and appreciate his true identity. Thus, when he won his second Masters in 1993, he felt completely fulfilled before he even reached the mountaintop. The journey was more important.

Again, maybe faith in God is not part of your belief system, but the point remains that one's belief becomes part of and determines our overall identity.

The Globetrotters are probably the only basketball players who have never lost a professional game. Being an exhibition team, they have toured the entire world and performed in front of millions of fans. However, an obscure fact is that they did once lose to the Washington Generals, in 1971, on a last-second shot. Let's just agree that they are "the winningest team in the world of sports."

At seven years old, Derick Grant witnessed his first Globetrotter experience and loved it so much that he started playing basketball the next day. His parents bought him a small hoop and he was all-in. He wanted to be a Globetrotter.

But where his career took a turn was in college.

He attended a small Division III school, the College of New Jersey. He started five games his freshman year and averaged an unspectacular, but respectable, five points per game. His sophomore year he progressed and started 15 games and averaged almost 15 points per contest.

He told his strength coach at the time that he wanted to be an All-American. The strength coach smirked and exclaimed that it was not possible. He elaborated and pointed out the obvious, which was that he hadn't even made the "all-conference team."

Some hinge moments are immediate, even though the effects are not seen until much later.

Derick Grant being told that he can't even make all-conference, let alone become an All-American, was the lightning strike that he needed. But his identity never wavered.

Derick Grant had a vision for himself and knew his identity was rooted in grace. We act according to our beliefs, so he acted as if he was already an All-American and Globetrotter and immediately *got to work.*

Derick did become conference player of the year and an All-American. He finished his college career with 1,542 career points. That achievement and love for the game propelled him to play professionally.

After his season was over, he went to exposure camps where he played in front of scouts, coaches, and agents. He went to six different camps and was rejected each time. Even though he was discouraged, his identity never wavered.

Only after he was denied on yet another camp in Scranton, Pennsylvania did a scout named Al Clocker notice and approach him. Derick managed to garner a spot on the Washington Generals, which was the team that played against the Harlem Globetrotters. The Globetrotters' coaches, staff, and other players saw him play every game for an entire season. Manny Jackson was the coach for the Globetrotters and gave him a try-out after his season with the Generals, and he earned his spot on the illustrious Harlem Globetrotters team.

Derick Grant would actually become "Dizzy" Grant. He played eight seasons for the team, playing in over seventy countries, impacting thousands of kid's lives the same way that he experienced it.

"Dizzy" was a ball-handling specialist, the one who would get kids spinning the ball on their finger in the middle of the court.

It was an impactful career.

He became the first player to ever make a 4-point shot for the Globetrotters and that basketball is immortalized in the Naismith Hall of Fame.

Even after his playing career was over, Derick Grant continued to work with others helping them with understanding their own true identity. His identity along his entire journey never wavered, and it was based on faith about "who" he was, but also "whose" he was.

Society wants us to believe that we are only as good as our results. Others want to tell us who we are and who we are not.

The University of Virginia basketball team showed perhaps the greatest team comeback of all time. They only lost one game in the ACC during the 2017-2018 season, finished 31-2, and also won the ACC tournament.

Then they became the first #1 seeded team ever to lose to a #16 seed.

The loss to UMBC was heartbreaking for them and the backlash they received for losing was sad, but proof that it's not about the *setback*, it's about the *comeback*. Three hundred and eighty-five days later, they won the national championship!

Puke
&
Rally.

What a feeling of redemption!

However, the headline that evening was, *"Virginia favored to repeat in 2020."*

Even if you're the best in the world, according to the world and society, it's not for very long.

The media aggressively perpetuates the notion of the mountaintop experience. It's like the media is selling a property at the top of the mountain that they themselves have never been to, but want to sell it to you.

Before the locker room has emptied and the stadium cleared out, the sports media finishes the broadcasts the same exact way. Confetti is still on the ground, the teams are still in the locker room, and the media has already started writing and talking about the next season.

The media have written numerous stories building up the season and championship game and then when it's over—nothing. It is immediately on to the next thing, the next season.

Our identity lasts way beyond when the scoreboard is turned off and everyone has gone home.

We are who we are when we are alone.

There will be good results and poor results, but our identity maintains steadfast during the ups and the downs. What we will remember most is the relationships and connections during our journey through each part of our lives.

Life does not get any easier as we age. It even often gets more complicated. But, what we do possess is better tools to facilitate the comeback.

There will be setbacks, and during each setback we just need to overcome the one mistake, misstep, or mishap. It's a bruise not a tattoo, and when we accept it, we can come back!

It does not mean there will only be one setback either. It means there will be setbacks in almost every endeavor that we do. It simply requires us to focus on our comeback from the current setback.

Puke
&
Rally!

CONTINUE THE JOURNEY

"Every end is a new beginning."—Marianne Williamson

YOU MUST BE awesome at never giving up!

You've made it this far and I thank you. To extend your results and impact, here are some resources to help you Puke & Rally and improve you and your team's mental toughness.

Books

If want to go at your own pace and still consume the information best suited for you. Check out all of our books at drrobbell.com/books

30-Day Mental Toughness Challenge

An intensive 30-day challenge that focuses on creating a better YOU and a better US. You'll receive a challenge everyday that will help you reach your own goal, create a bulletproof routine, and improve your most important relationships. Details at noonegetstherealone.com

15 Minutes of Mental Toughness Podcast

We interviews experts, coaches, and athletes about mental toughness and their Hinge moments. You'll get inspired and receive amazing strength, hope, and experience, from people who have Puked & Rallied. Listen and Subscribe on Apple podcasts

Keynote Speaking and Workshops

One of my favorite things is being able to spread the word and inspire, energize, and treat teams and organizations. Whether this is from the stage, boardroom, or locker room, being able to teach mental toughness is the passion. You'll know the impact when your team performs it's best when it matters THE MOST. Details at drrobbell.com/keynote-speaker

Coaching

A coach is someone who takes you where you want to go. This is intensive and personalized coaching for corporate athletes, elite, and professional athletes. If you want to puke & rally and to seize your Hinge moment and significance in life, schedule a call. Drrobbell.com

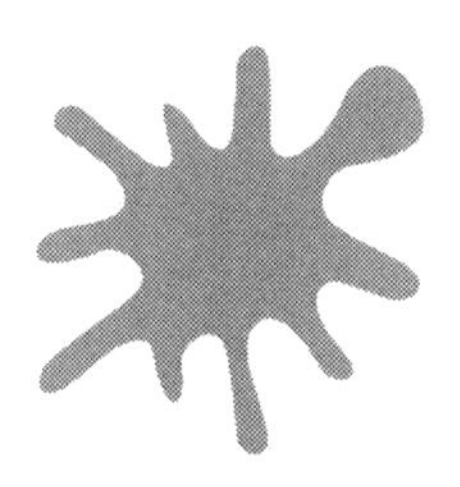

REFERENCES

1. Hardy, L. (1990). A catastrophe model of performance in sport. In J. G. Jones & L. Hardy (Eds.), *Wiley series in human performance and cognition. Stress and performance in sport* (p. 81–106). John Wiley & Sons.

2. Larimer, M. E., Palmer, R. S., & Marlatt, G. A. (1999). Relapse prevention: An overview of Marlatt's cognitive-behavioral model. *Alcohol Research & Health,* 23(2), 151–160.

3. Martin, L. R., Williams, S. L., Haskard, K. B., & Dimatteo, M. R. (2005). The challenge of patient adherence. *Therapeutics and clinical risk management,* 1(3), 189–199.

4. Metzner, J. L., & Fellner, J. (2010). Solitary confinement and mental illness in U.S. prisons: A challenge for medical ethics. *Journal of the American Academy of Psychiatry and the Law, 38*(1), 104–108.

5. Harlow, H. F., Dodsworth, R. O., & Harlow, M. K. (1965). Total social isolation in monkeys. *Proceedings of the National Academy of Sciences of the United States of America, 54*(1), 90–97.

6. Frankl, V. E. (1984). *Man's search for meaning: An introduction to logotherapy.* New York: Simon & Schuster.

7. Schawbel, D. (2018). *Back to Human: How Great Leaders Create Connection in the Age of Isolation.* Hachette Book Group.

8. V. A. Rakov and M. A. Uman, (1998). Review and evaluation of lightning return stroke models including some aspects of their application" *IEEE Transactions on Electromagnetic Compatibility*, vol. 40, no. 4, pp. 403-426.

9. Nag, A., and Rakov, V. A. (2012), Positive lightning: An overview, new observations, and inferences, *J. Geophys. Res.*, 117, D08109.

10. Kissel, C., (August 9, 2016) "Dubstep violinist" Lindsey Stirling is more popular than lady gaga (sort of). *LA Weekly.*

11. Leive, C. (December, 7, 2015). Meet Lindsey Stirling, the Highest-Earning Female YouTuber. *Glamour Magazine.*

12. Moraski, L., (December 19, 2018). 'America's Got Talent' Asked Lindsey Stirling To Compete Again. Here's What She Said. *Huffpost.com Entertainment.*

13. Kessler, M. (June 21, 2019) Kalin Bennett Has Autism—And He's A Div. I Basketball Player. *WBUR- Only A Game.*

14. Smith, S. (January 1, 2020). Eagles running back Boston Scott explains what Joshua 1:9 means to him. *The Christian Post.*

15. Campbell, J. (1999) *Recovering Benjamin Franklin: an exploration of a life of science and service.* Open Court Publishing.

16. Lesser, C. (August 24, 2018). The Centuries-Old Japanese Tradition of Mending Broken Ceramics with Gold. *Artsy.net.*

17. Holman Bible Publishers. (2009). Acts 9:5. In *Holy Bible: Holman Christian Standard Version.* Nashville, TN.

18. Holman Bible Publishers. (2009). Acts 9:15-17. In *Holy Bible: Holman Christian Standard Version*. Nashville, TN.

19. Meier, A. (February 16, 2017). An Artist Mends Cracks in the Sidewalk with Gold. *Hyperallergic*

20. McLaughlin, C. (2018, December 20). Ravens Tight End Hayden Hurst Shares His Journey With Anxiety and Depression. *Baltimore Magazine.*

21. Holman Bible Publishers. (2009). Mark 11: 22-24. In *Holy Bible: Holman Christian Standard Version*. Nashville, TN.

22. Lite, J. (2008, December 10). Death on Mount Everest: The perils of the descent. *Scientific American.*

23. D'Amato, G. (2005, September 17). Brett Favre: The Making of a Legend. *Milwaukee- Journal Sentinel.* Retrieved from jsonline.com.

24. Packers' Super Bowl XXXI Victory To Be Featured On NFL Network's 'America's Game'. (2006, December 17). Retrieved from https://www.packers.com.

25. Ware, B. (2019). *The top five regrets of the dying: a life transformed by the dearly departing*. Carlsbad, CA: Hay House Inc.

26. Nyad, D. (2016). *Find a way: the inspiring story of one woman's pursuit of a lifelong dream*. New York: Vintage Books, a division of Penguin Random House LLC.

27. Shields, E. (2017, October 9). How Secretariat gave the Canadians something to remember for ever: Topics: Woodbine Racetrack, Secretariat, A.P. Indy, Canadian International.

28. Oller, R. (2003, April 14). Golfer Bernhard Langer Finds His Master at the Masters. Retrieved from https://www.crosswalk.com/faith/spiritual-life/golfer-bernhard-langer-finds-his-master-at-the-masters-1195170.html

Made in the USA
Monee, IL
06 November 2023